Scotland Travel Guide 2025

Isle of Skye Edinburgh,Glasgow,The Highlands,Untamed Wilderness,Festival Fringe,Outdoor Adventures.

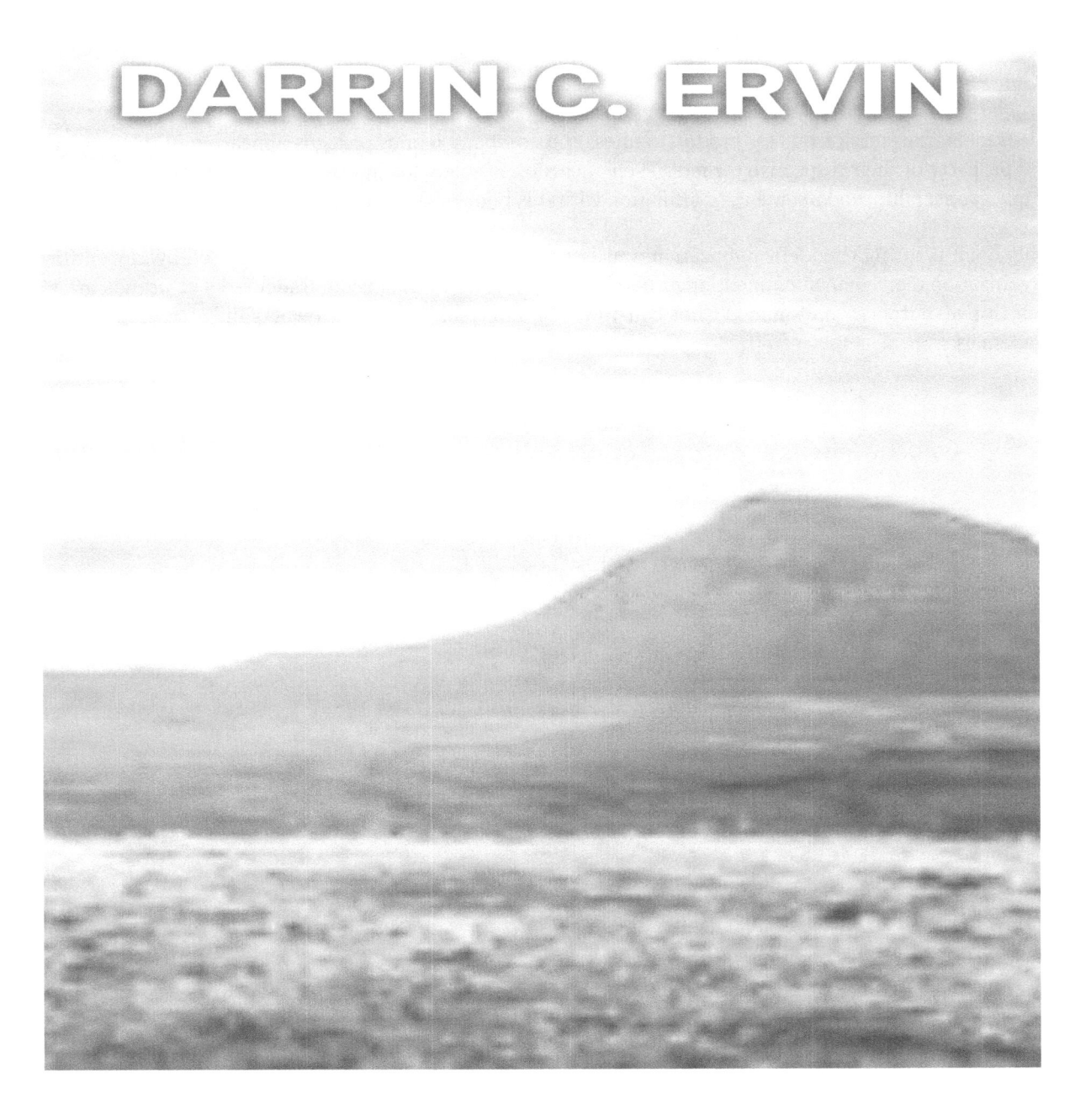

DARRIN C. ERVIN

Copyright © 2025 by Darrin C. Ervin. All rights reserved.

No part of this publication may be reproduced, distributed, or transmitted in any form or by any means, including photocopying, recording, or other electronic or mechanical methods, without the prior written permission of the author, except in the case of brief quotations used in book reviews and other non-commercial uses as permitted by copyright law.

This book is a work of nonfiction. While every effort has been made to ensure accuracy, the author and publisher assume no responsibility for errors, omissions, or changes in details after the time of publication. The information in this guide is for general purposes only and should not be used as a substitute for professional advice or official travel guidelines.

Trademark Disclaimer

All trademarks, service marks, product names, and company names or logos appearing in this book are the property of their respective owners. Their inclusion is solely for informational purposes and does not imply sponsorship, endorsement, or affiliation with this book or the author.

This book is an independent publication and is not authorized, sponsored, or endorsed by any entities, organizations, or companies mentioned herein. Any references to specific trademarks or brands are for descriptive purposes only and do not constitute or imply any claim of ownership or rights to those trademarks.

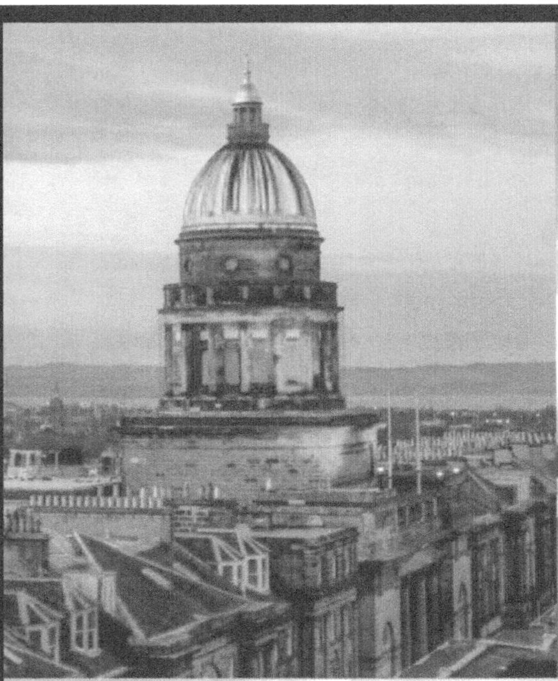
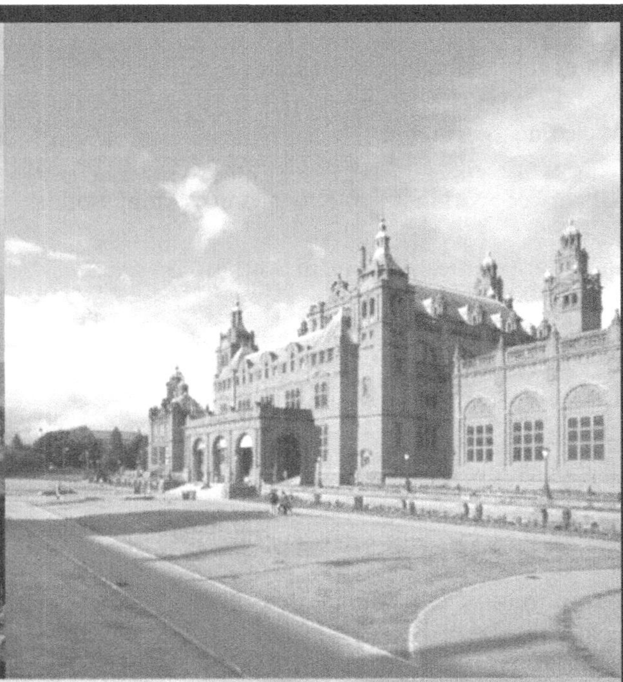
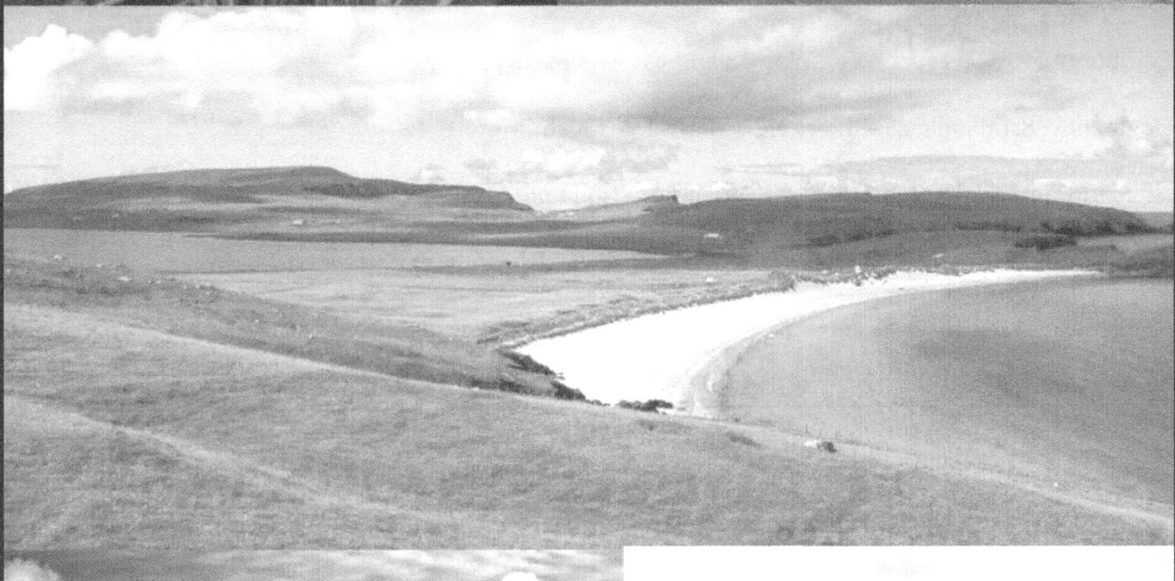
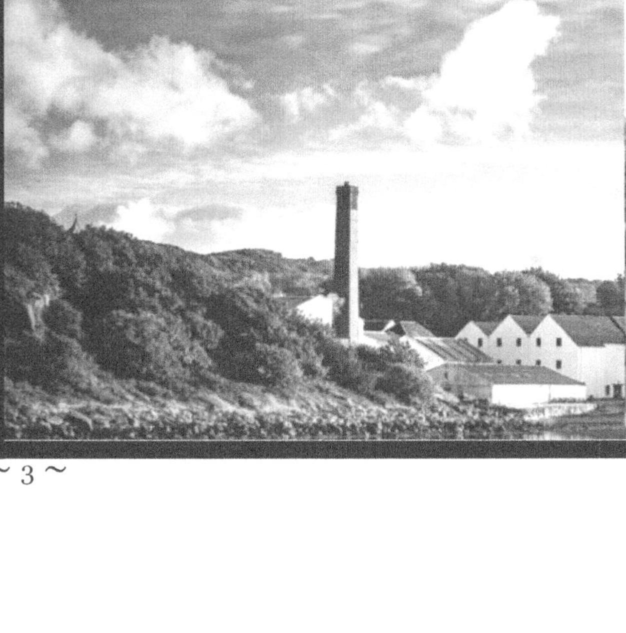
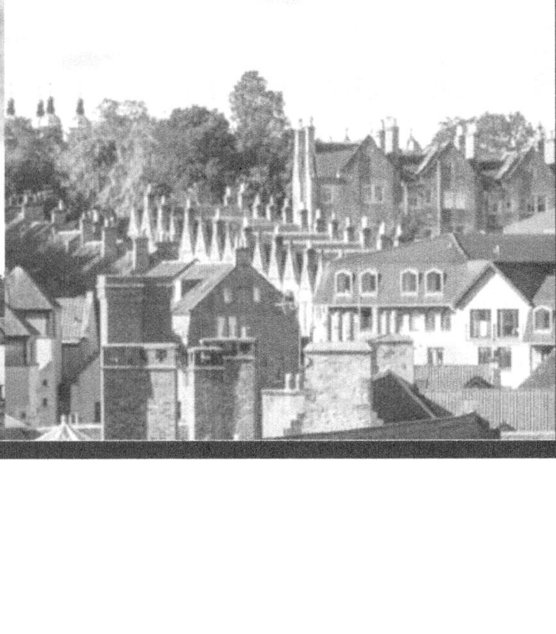

Table of Content

Chapter 1: Introduction to Scotland — 7
- Welcome to Scotland — 7
- History of Scotland: Key Events and Turning Points — 8

Chapter 2: Top Destinations in Scotland — 10
- Edinburgh: Scotland's Enchanting Capital — 10
- Glasgow: Scotland's Dynamic Cultural Hub — 11
- The Highlands: Scotland's Untamed Wilderness — 13
- Isle of Skye: Scotland's Enchanting Island — 15
- St. Andrews: The Birthplace of Golf and Coastal Beauty — 16

Chapter 3: Festivals and Events — 19
- Edinburgh Festival Fringe: The World's Largest Arts Festival — 19
- Hogmanay: Scotland's Legendary New Year's Eve Celebration — 21
- Highland Games: A Celebration of Scottish Tradition and Strength — 23
- The Royal Edinburgh Military Tattoo: A Spectacular Celebration of Music and Tradition — 26
- Isle of Skye Music Festival: A Harmonious Celebration of Music and Scenic Beauty — 29

Chapter 4: Outdoor Adventures in Scotland — 32
- Hiking in the Highlands and National Parks — 32
- National Parks Hiking: Cairngorms National Park and Loch Lomond & The Trossachs National Park — 35
- Cycling and Biking Routes in Scotland — 42
- Whale Watching in the Hebrides — 45

Chapter 5: Cultural and Historical Attractions — 48
- Edinburgh Castle and the Royal Mile — 48
- Urquhart Castle and Loch Ness — 50
- The Falkirk Wheel — 52

    Scottish National Gallery   54

Chapter 6: Unique Scottish Experiences   57

    Ghost Tours in Edinburgh   57

    Stargazing in Galloway Forest   61

    Whisky Distillery Tours and Tastings in Scotland   64

Chapter 7: Scottish Cuisine and Dining   67

    Traditional Scottish Dishes: Haggis, Cullen Skink, and Shortbread   67

    Best pubs and restaurants across Scotland   69

    Whisky Tastings and Food Pairings in Scotland   71

    Exploring Local Markets and Food Festivals in Scotland   74

Chapter 8: Accommodation in Scotland   78

    Luxury hotels and historic castles   78

    Camping and glamping options   79

Chapter 9: Getting Around Scotland   82

    Public Transportation in Scotland: Trains, Buses, and Ferries   82

    Renting a Car for the Highland Routes and Isle of Skye   84

    Cycling and Walking Paths for Exploration in Scotland   87

    Tips for Driving in Rural and Remote Areas of Scotland   89

Chapter 10: Sample Itinerary and Travel Tips   93

    7-Day Itinerary: Edinburgh, Stirling, Glasgow, The Highlands, Isle of Skye, and St. Andrews   93

    How to Plan Your Trip to Scotland for Different Seasons   97

    Packing Tips and Essential Items to Bring for Your Trip to Scotland   100

    Navigating Scotland's Weather and Terrain   103

    Navigating Scotland's Terrain   105

Chapter 11. Conclusion   108

Reflecting on Scotland's Unforgettable Experience: A Journey Through Time, Nature, and Culture 108

Bonus 109

Travel Journal 110

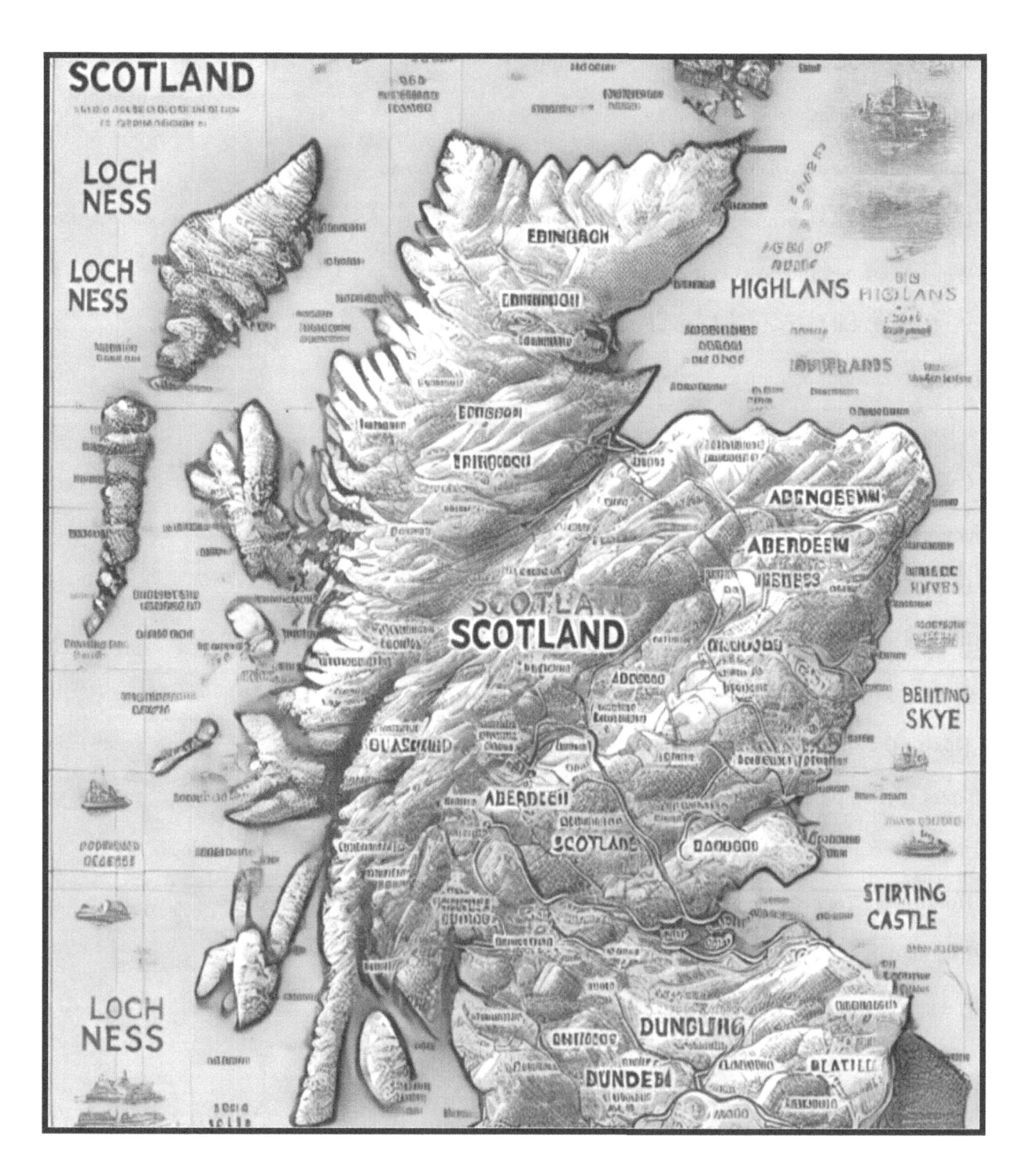

Chapter 1: Introduction to Scotland

Welcome to Scotland

As I stepped off the plane, a brisk breeze carried the scent of rain and earth—an unmistakable sign that I had arrived in Scotland. My first glimpse of the country felt like stepping into a postcard: rolling green hills stretching into the horizon, dotted with grazing sheep and ancient stone walls. Even in that fleeting moment, I could sense the timelessness of this land—a place where history and nature coexist in perfect harmony.

Scotland greeted me with an open heart, and every step I took felt like uncovering a treasure. My journey began in Edinburgh, where the cobbled streets of the Royal Mile echoed with stories of kings, queens, and rebels. I remember standing before the majestic Edinburgh Castle, its towering walls a silent witness to centuries of history. As the sun dipped behind the city, I climbed Arthur's Seat, the extinct volcano that offers a panoramic view of Scotland's capital. From up there, the city unfolded like a tapestry: gothic spires, Georgian architecture, and beyond, the shimmering waters of the Firth of Forth.

But it wasn't just the landscapes and landmarks that left an imprint on my heart—it was the people. The warmth of a stranger's smile, the lilting cadence of the Scottish accent, and the countless "cheers" shared over a pint of local ale made me feel like I belonged, even as a visitor.

Then came the Highlands. Driving through Glencoe was like stepping into a dream—towering peaks shrouded in mist, deep glens carved by ancient glaciers, and a silence so profound it felt sacred. One morning, I rose early to watch the sunrise over Loch Ness. The lake was still and mysterious, the water mirroring the pastel hues of dawn. I didn't spot Nessie, but the moment felt magical nonetheless, as if the loch itself was guarding secrets only it could tell.

Scotland's charm is in its contrasts. In bustling Glasgow, I discovered a vibrant arts scene, quirky cafés, and the city's beating heart in its music. On the Isle of Skye, I stood in awe before the Fairy Pools, where crystal-clear waters cascade through a rugged landscape. Each corner of Scotland offered a different kind of wonder, from the medieval ruins of St. Andrews to the remote beauty of the Orkney Islands.

And then there was the food. I'll admit, I was hesitant to try haggis at first, but with one bite, I was a convert. Paired with neeps and tatties (turnips and potatoes), it was a meal as hearty and honest as the country itself. I also indulged in buttery shortbread, freshly caught salmon, and, of course, a dram of whisky that warmed me from the inside out.

Every traveler has a moment when a destination truly takes hold of their heart. For me, it was during a ceilidh, a traditional Scottish dance. With fiddles and bagpipes filling the room, I found myself swept into a lively reel, laughing and twirling with people I'd only just met. It was in that moment I realized Scotland wasn't just a place to visit—it was a place to feel alive.

As I write this, I can still hear the haunting melody of a lone piper on the windswept cliffs of Dunnottar Castle. Scotland isn't just a destination; it's an experience—a journey that weaves its way into your soul and leaves you longing to return. So, welcome to Scotland, a land where every corner has a story, and every visitor becomes part of its tale.

Here's a rewritten version of Scotland's history with the main events highlighted clearly in a narrative format:

History of Scotland: Key Events and Turning Points

Scotland's history is one of resilience and transformation, shaped by a series of pivotal events that have defined its identity over millennia.

Prehistoric Beginnings

Scotland's story begins over 10,000 years ago during the Mesolithic era, with early human settlements along its coasts. By the Neolithic period, remarkable sites like Skara Brae in Orkney and the Callanish Standing Stones emerged, revealing sophisticated communities and rituals.

The Roman Encounter (1st-4th Century AD)

Although the Romans never fully conquered Scotland—known to them as Caledonia—they built Hadrian's Wall and later the Antonine Wall to mark their northern frontier. Scottish tribes, particularly the fierce Caledonians, resisted Roman advances, showcasing the early defiance of its people.

Formation of the Kingdom of Alba (9th Century)

The unification of the Picts and Scots under King Kenneth MacAlpin in the 9th century marked a defining moment in Scotland's history. This union established the Kingdom of Alba, the foundation of modern Scotland.

Viking Age and Norse Influence (8th-13th Century)

From the 8th century, Viking raids and settlements shaped Scotland's coastal regions, particularly in the Orkney and Shetland Islands. While the Norse left a lasting cultural imprint, Scottish kings eventually reclaimed these territories.

The Wars of Independence (1296–1357)

Scotland's fight for sovereignty against English rule became legendary during this period. Key events included:

- 1297: William Wallace's victory at the Battle of Stirling Bridge.

- 1314: Robert the Bruce's triumph at the Battle of Bannockburn, securing Scotland's independence.

- 1320: The Declaration of Arbroath, a powerful statement of Scotland's right to freedom.

The Stewart Dynasty (1371–1603)

The Stewart family came to power with Robert II in 1371, overseeing Scotland's cultural and political growth. The Auld Alliance with France strengthened ties against England, and the Scottish Reformation in the 16th century brought significant religious changes, replacing Catholicism with Protestantism.

Union of the Crowns (1603)

In 1603, James VI of Scotland became James I of England, uniting the two crowns under a single monarch. However, Scotland retained its distinct parliament and laws during this period.

The Act of Union (1707)

The formal union of Scotland and England into Great Britain in 1707 ended Scotland's parliamentary independence. While it brought economic opportunities, it also fueled widespread resentment and uprisings.

The Jacobite Risings (1688–1746)

The Jacobite movement sought to restore the exiled Stuart monarchy. Key moments included:

- 1715: The first major Jacobite uprising, led by the Earl of Mar.

- 1746: The Battle of Culloden, the final defeat of the Jacobites, leading to the suppression of Highland culture and the Highland Clearances.

The Industrial Revolution (18th-19th Century)

Scotland became a hub of innovation, trade, and industry during the Industrial Revolution. Cities like Glasgow thrived as centers of shipbuilding and commerce, while the Scottish Enlightenment, led by figures such as Adam Smith and David Hume, left a profound intellectual legacy.

Devolution and Modern Scotland (20th-21st Century)

In the 20th century, Scotland experienced a cultural revival and political change. The establishment of the Scottish Parliament in 1999 granted greater autonomy, marking a new chapter in its history. Today, debates over independence and Scotland's role in the United Kingdom continue to shape its future.

Chapter 2: Top Destinations in Scotland

Edinburgh: Scotland's Enchanting Capital

Edinburgh, Scotland's capital, is a city of striking contrasts where ancient history meets modern vibrancy. With its cobbled streets, dramatic skyline, and rich cultural heritage, Edinburgh offers an unforgettable experience for travelers.

What to Explore in Edinburgh

Edinburgh Castle dominates the city's skyline, perched on Castle Rock. Explore the Crown Jewels, the Stone of Destiny, and enjoy panoramic views of the city.

The Royal Mile is a historic stretch linking Edinburgh Castle to the Palace of Holyroodhouse. It's filled with charming shops, historic landmarks, and quaint alleyways known as "closes."

Arthur's Seat, an extinct volcano, offers stunning views of the city and surrounding landscape. It's a must-visit for outdoor enthusiasts.

The National Museum of Scotland showcases Scotland's history, culture, and natural world with exhibits ranging from ancient artifacts to cutting-edge technology. Entry is free.

The Scottish Parliament and Holyrood Palace are iconic landmarks, with the modern Parliament building contrasting the historic Holyrood Palace, the Queen's official residence in Scotland.

Calton Hill is known for its collection of monuments, including the National Monument and Nelson's Monument, and is perfect for photography and sunset views.

Princes Street Gardens, nestled in the shadow of Edinburgh Castle, is a tranquil spot for a stroll or a picnic.

For a spookier experience, explore the Edinburgh Vaults and Mary King's Close, where ghost tours uncover the city's underground history.

What to Expect in Edinburgh

Edinburgh is a fusion of old and new, with the historic Old Town offering a medieval layout and the elegant New Town showcasing Georgian architecture.

Seasonal events, such as the Edinburgh Festival Fringe in August and the Hogmanay celebrations at New Year, add to the city's allure.

The vibrant nightlife includes traditional pubs, modern cocktail bars, and live music venues.

Edinburgh's weather can be cool and unpredictable, so packing layers is essential, even in summer.

How to Get to Edinburgh

Edinburgh Airport (EDI) serves international and domestic flights. Located about 8 miles (13 km) from the city center, it's easily accessible by airport buses, trams, or taxis.

Waverley Station, in the heart of the city, connects Edinburgh to major UK cities like London, Glasgow, and Manchester.

Budget-friendly bus options like National Express and Megabus link Edinburgh to other cities across the UK.

For those driving, Edinburgh is accessible via major motorways, though parking can be expensive and limited, making public transport a convenient alternative.

Cost of Visiting Edinburgh

Accommodation options vary to suit all budgets. Hostels and budget hotels start from £20–£50 per night, while mid-range hotels and guesthouses range from £70–£150 per night. Luxury accommodations can cost between £200–£500 per night.

For food and drinks, budget meals cost around £10–£15 per person, while mid-range restaurants range from £20–£40 per person. A pint of beer in a pub typically costs £4–£6.

Attractions such as Edinburgh Castle and Holyrood Palace have admission fees of £18–£22 and £17, respectively. However, many sites, like the National Museum of Scotland, offer free entry.

Transportation within Edinburgh is affordable, with single bus or tram rides costing around £2 and day passes for unlimited travel starting at £4.50.

Edinburgh is a city that captures the hearts of its visitors with its historic charm, cultural vibrancy, and warm hospitality. Whether you're hiking Arthur's Seat or uncovering its underground secrets, Edinburgh promises an adventure like no other.

Glasgow: Scotland's Dynamic Cultural Hub

Glasgow, Scotland's largest city, is renowned for its dynamic blend of culture, history, and modernity. From its vibrant music scene to its striking architecture, Glasgow offers visitors an unforgettable experience filled with warmth, creativity, and energy.

What to Explore in Glasgow

Kelvingrove Art Gallery and Museum is a cultural treasure trove featuring diverse exhibits, including fine art, natural history, and local heritage. Admission is free, making it a must-visit.

The Riverside Museum, Glasgow's transport museum, showcases an impressive collection of vintage vehicles, ships, and interactive exhibits. Step aboard the Tall Ship docked nearby for a unique maritime experience.

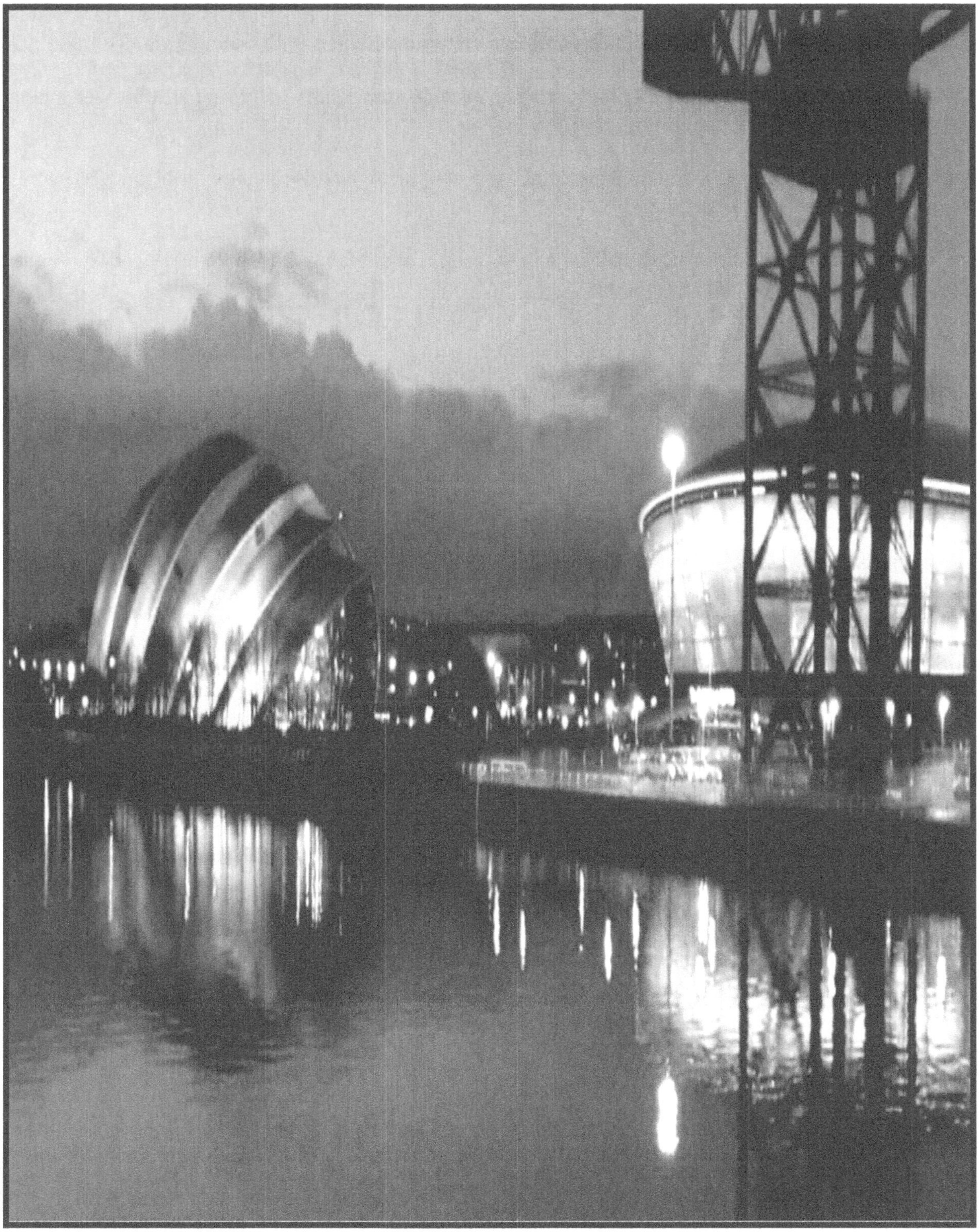

George Square, the city's central hub, is surrounded by stunning Victorian buildings and serves as a great starting point for exploring the city.

The Glasgow Cathedral, a magnificent medieval structure, is steeped in history and offers a serene atmosphere for reflection. Nearby, the Necropolis is a Victorian cemetery with stunning views of the city.

The People's Palace and Winter Gardens provide insights into Glasgow's social history, set amidst beautiful gardens perfect for a relaxing stroll.

Buchanan Street, part of Glasgow's "Style Mile," is a shopper's paradise filled with high-street stores, designer boutiques, and bustling cafes.

For music lovers, the Barrowland Ballroom and King Tut's Wah Wah Hut are legendary venues showcasing Glasgow's vibrant music scene.

What to Expect in Glasgow

Glasgow is a city of contrasts, blending historic landmarks with modern developments. Its industrial heritage is visible alongside its thriving cultural and artistic offerings.

Expect a lively atmosphere, especially in its bustling nightlife spots, trendy neighborhoods, and friendly pubs.

Glasgow is also a UNESCO City of Music, hosting live performances across genres almost daily.

The city's weather is similar to the rest of Scotland—unpredictable—so dressing in layers and carrying an umbrella is always a good idea.

How to Get to Glasgow

Glasgow Airport (GLA) connects the city to international and domestic destinations. It is about 8 miles (13 km) from the city center, with buses and taxis providing easy access.

Glasgow Central Station is the main hub for train travel, offering frequent services to other Scottish cities and the rest of the UK, including Edinburgh and London.

For bus travel, Buchanan Bus Station is the city's primary terminal, connecting Glasgow to nearby towns and cities at budget-friendly prices.

Driving into Glasgow is convenient via major motorways, though parking in the city center can be limited and costly.

Cost of Visiting Glasgow

Accommodation options range from budget hostels costing £15–£40 per night to mid-range hotels priced at £60–£120 per night. Luxury hotels and serviced apartments are available from £150 upwards.

Dining out in Glasgow is affordable, with casual meals starting at £10–£15 per person and mid-range restaurants offering meals at £20–£35. The city's vibrant street food scene provides even more budget-friendly options.

Attractions such as the Kelvingrove Museum, Riverside Museum, and Glasgow Cathedral offer free entry, while other attractions like the Glasgow Science Centre charge fees ranging from £10–£15.

Transportation within the city is affordable, with single bus or subway rides costing approximately £1.80–£2.50. Day passes for unlimited travel start at £4.

Glasgow's unique mix of cultural heritage, modern innovation, and warm community spirit makes it an essential stop on any Scottish adventure. Whether you're exploring its historic landmarks, diving into its artistic scene, or enjoying its vibrant nightlife, Glasgow has something for everyone.

The Highlands: Scotland's Untamed Wilderness

The Highlands, a vast and breathtaking region in Scotland, is a land of rugged mountains, tranquil lochs, and charming villages. Known for its rich history and dramatic landscapes, it offers visitors an unforgettable escape into nature, culture, and adventure.

What to Explore in the Highlands

Loch Ness, home to the legendary Nessie, is a must-visit. Take a boat cruise, explore Urquhart Castle, or simply soak in the mystical beauty of the loch.

Ben Nevis, the UK's highest mountain, offers incredible hiking opportunities and stunning panoramic views for adventurous visitors.

The Isle of Skye, often called "Scotland in miniature," is renowned for its dramatic cliffs, Fairy Pools, and the Quiraing's unique rock formations.

Glen Coe, known for its haunting beauty, is a paradise for hikers and photographers. It also has a rich, tragic history that echoes through its stunning landscapes.

The Cairngorms National Park is perfect for outdoor enthusiasts, offering activities like hiking, skiing, and wildlife spotting. Look out for red squirrels and golden eagles.

Eilean Donan Castle, perched on a small island where three lochs meet, is one of Scotland's most iconic and photographed castles.

The North Coast 500 (NC500) is a scenic driving route that takes you through the Highlands' most spectacular landscapes, dotted with beaches, castles, and quaint villages.

What to Expect in the Highlands

The Highlands are a remote and sparsely populated region, offering an authentic sense of tranquility and escape from urban life.

Expect to encounter friendly locals, many of whom speak Scots Gaelic alongside English.

The weather can be unpredictable, so prepare for rain and wind even in summer. However, the dramatic skies add to the region's charm.

The Highlands are rich in history and folklore, with tales of clan battles, Jacobite uprisings, and mythical creatures woven into the landscape.

How to Get to the Highlands

Inverness Airport (INV) serves as a gateway to the Highlands, offering flights from major UK cities like London, Edinburgh, and Manchester.

Inverness is also accessible by train, with direct services from Glasgow, Edinburgh, and other cities.

Bus services, such as Citylink, connect Inverness and other Highland towns to the rest of Scotland.

Driving is one of the best ways to explore the Highlands, allowing flexibility to reach remote areas. Car rentals are widely available in cities like Inverness.

Cost of Visiting the Highlands

Accommodation varies from budget-friendly hostels and B&Bs starting at £20–£50 per night to luxurious lodges and hotels priced at £150 and above.

Dining options include cozy pubs and local restaurants where meals typically cost £10–£25 per person. Try traditional Highland fare like haggis, fresh seafood, and venison.

Attractions like castles and visitor centers charge entrance fees ranging from £5–£15, while outdoor activities such as hiking and exploring lochs are free.

Transportation costs depend on your mode of travel, but fuel costs should be considered if driving, as distances between destinations can be significant.

The Highlands offer a magical blend of natural beauty, cultural heritage, and outdoor adventure. Whether you're exploring ancient castles, hiking rugged peaks, or searching for Nessie, the Highlands promise an unforgettable journey into Scotland's wild heart.

Isle of Skye: Scotland's Enchanting Island

The Isle of Skye, often referred to as "Scotland in miniature," is a captivating destination that epitomizes the country's natural beauty and mythical charm. From dramatic cliffs and sparkling lochs to ancient castles and quaint villages, Skye offers a unique blend of adventure and serenity.

What to Explore on the Isle of Skye

The Fairy Pools, nestled in Glen Brittle, are a series of crystal-clear blue pools and waterfalls perfect for a scenic walk or a chilly wild swim.

The Quiraing, a dramatic landslip on the Trotternish Ridge, offers surreal landscapes and hiking trails with breathtaking views.

The Old Man of Storr, a striking rock formation, is one of Skye's most iconic landmarks. The hike to the top rewards visitors with panoramic views of the surrounding lochs and hills.

Dunvegan Castle and Gardens, the seat of the MacLeod clan, is steeped in history and set amidst lush gardens. A boat trip here offers the chance to spot seals basking on the nearby rocks.

Neist Point Lighthouse, perched on a rugged cliff, is an excellent spot for sunset views and wildlife watching, including dolphins and sea birds.

Portree, the island's charming capital, is famous for its colorful harbor, lively pubs, and local crafts.

Talisker Distillery offers a taste of Skye's world-famous single malt whisky. Take a tour to learn about its production and enjoy a sample.

What to Expect on the Isle of Skye

The Isle of Skye is a haven for outdoor enthusiasts and photographers, with its dramatic scenery and ever-changing weather creating magical photo opportunities.

Expect a peaceful atmosphere, especially in its remote areas, though popular sites like the Fairy Pools and Old Man of Storr can get busy during peak seasons.

The island is rich in folklore, with tales of fairies, giants, and ancient clans adding an enchanting dimension to its landscapes.

Wildlife is abundant, with chances to spot otters, seals, eagles, and even whales along the coastline.

The weather is unpredictable, with rain showers and strong winds common even in summer, so waterproof clothing is essential.

How to Get to the Isle of Skye

The Skye Bridge connects the island to mainland Scotland, making it easily accessible by car. The journey from Inverness to Skye takes approximately 2.5 hours.

Buses operated by Citylink connect Skye to major cities like Inverness, Glasgow, and Edinburgh.

For a scenic alternative, the Mallaig-Armadale ferry provides a short and picturesque crossing from the mainland.

If you're traveling by train, the nearest station is Kyle of Lochalsh, from where you can continue to Skye by bus or car.

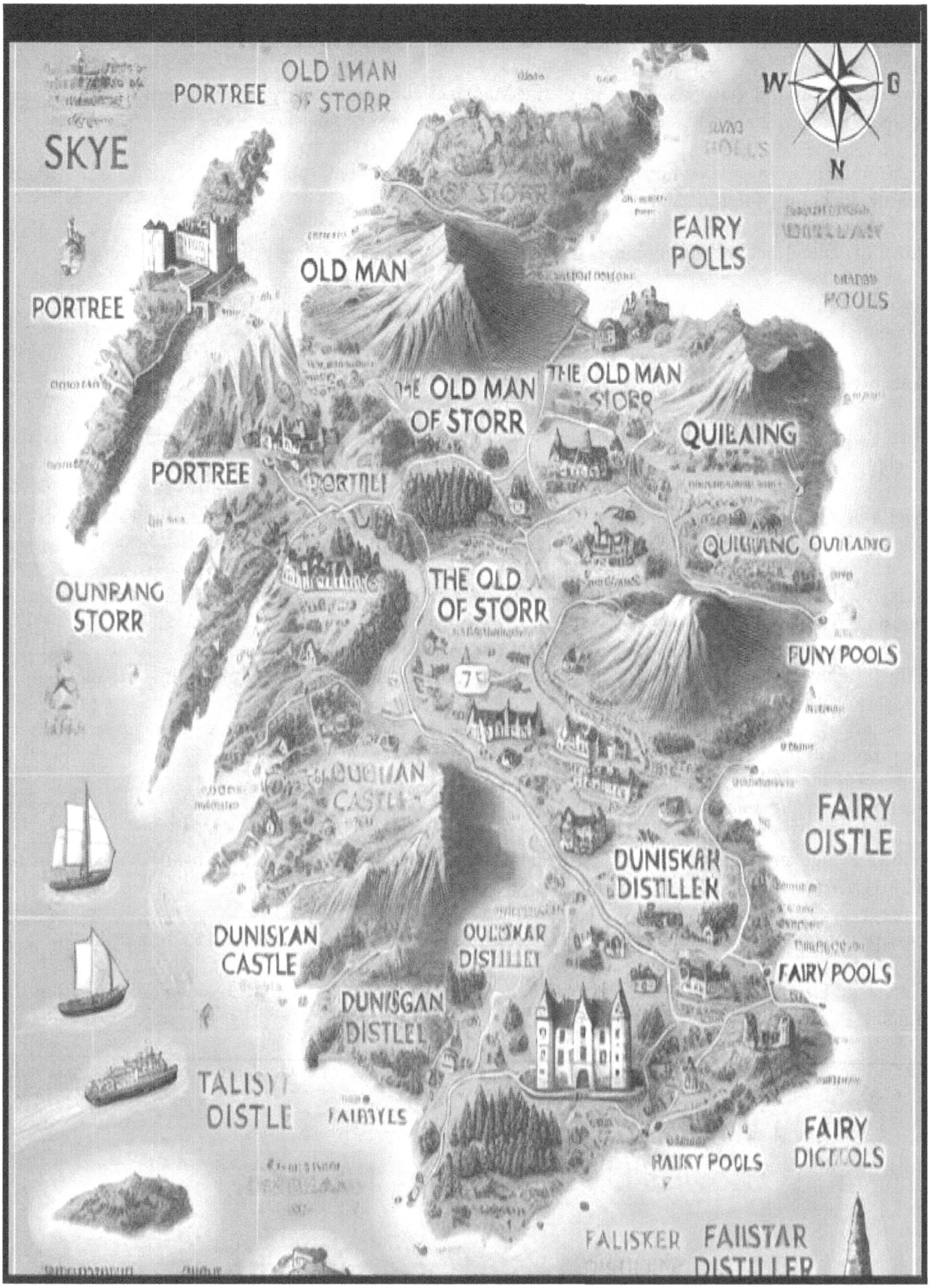
PORTREE
SKYE
W
N
FAIRY POLLS
OLD MAN
PORTREE
OLD MAN OF STORR
QUILAING
PORTREE
QUIRANG
OUNRANG STORR
THE OLD OF STORR
FUNY POOLS
FAIRY OISTLE
DUNISKAR DISTILLEN
DUNISKAN CASTLE
FAIRY POOLS
DUNISGAN DISTLEL
TALISIT DISTLE
FAIRY DICTOLS
FALISKER
FAIISTAR DISTILLER

Cost of Visiting the Isle of Skye

Accommodation on Skye ranges from budget-friendly hostels and guesthouses priced at £20–£60 per night to luxurious hotels and lodges costing upwards of £150.

Dining options include cozy pubs, seafood restaurants, and cafes where meals typically cost between £10 and £30. Don't miss the chance to sample fresh local seafood and traditional Scottish dishes.

Many outdoor activities, such as hiking and exploring natural attractions, are free. Entry fees for places like Dunvegan Castle range from £10–£15.

Car rentals are available on the mainland for exploring the island at your own pace. Fuel costs should be factored in, as public transport on the island is limited.

The Isle of Skye's dramatic landscapes, rich history, and welcoming spirit make it a dream destination for travelers seeking natural beauty and adventure. Whether you're exploring its iconic landmarks or simply soaking in its tranquil charm, Skye is a place you'll never forget.

St. Andrews: The Birthplace of Golf and Coastal Beauty

St. Andrews, a historic town on Scotland's east coast, is renowned for its ancient university, stunning beaches, and being the home of golf. This charming town offers a delightful mix of history, natural beauty, and vibrant culture, making it a must-visit destination.

What to Explore in St. Andrews

The Old Course at St. Andrews is a pilgrimage site for golf enthusiasts worldwide. Even if you're not a golfer, a visit to the iconic Swilcan Bridge and the British Golf Museum is a must.

St. Andrews Cathedral, once the largest church in Scotland, now stands as a majestic ruin. Climb St. Rule's Tower for panoramic views of the town and coastline.

St. Andrews Castle, perched on a cliff, offers a glimpse into medieval life and features fascinating attractions like the underground mine and the bottle dungeon.

West Sands Beach, famous for its appearance in the film Chariots of Fire, is perfect for a leisurely walk, a picnic, or even kite flying.

The University of St. Andrews, Scotland's oldest university, boasts beautiful architecture, cobbled streets, and historical significance. Visit the quad and explore the university's museums and library.

St. Andrews Botanic Garden is a serene escape with beautifully landscaped gardens, glasshouses, and a variety of plant collections.

What to Expect in St. Andrews

The town offers a peaceful and intimate atmosphere, with a blend of historic charm and modern vibrancy.

Expect to see a mix of students, locals, and tourists, especially during the academic year or when major golf tournaments are held.

St. Andrews has a rich cultural heritage, with historic buildings, museums, and plenty of stories about its ties to Scotland's monarchy and religious history.

The town's compact size makes it easy to explore on foot, and its picturesque streets are lined with boutique shops, cafes, and restaurants.

The coastal setting provides breathtaking views, with beaches, cliffs, and the North Sea adding to the town's allure.

How to Get to St. Andrews

The closest airport is Edinburgh Airport, located about 50 miles away. From there, you can take a bus or train to St. Andrews.

Leuchars is the nearest train station, approximately six miles from the town. Regular buses and taxis connect Leuchars to St. Andrews.

Direct bus services, such as those operated by Stagecoach, link St. Andrews to Edinburgh, Dundee, and other cities.

Driving to St. Andrews is another option, with ample parking available in the town.

Cost of Visiting St. Andrews

Accommodation ranges from cozy B&Bs and guesthouses starting at £50 per night to luxury hotels like the Old Course Hotel, which can cost over £200 per night.

Dining options include casual cafes, traditional pubs, and fine dining establishments. Meals typically cost between £10 and £30 per person.

Entry fees to attractions such as St. Andrews Castle and Cathedral range from £6 to £12, while many outdoor attractions, like the beaches, are free to enjoy.

Golf enthusiasts should budget for green fees, which can range from £25 at smaller courses to over £200 at the Old Course.

Local bus fares and taxi services are reasonably priced, and the town's walkability makes it easy to save on transportation costs.

St. Andrews combines historic allure, coastal beauty, and a rich golfing legacy to create an unforgettable experience for every visitor. Whether you're exploring medieval ruins, strolling along the beach, or teeing off at a world-famous golf course, this charming town has something for everyone.

Chapter 3: Festivals and Events

Edinburgh Festival Fringe: The World's Largest Arts Festival

The Edinburgh Festival Fringe is a vibrant and world-renowned event that takes place every August in the Scottish capital. Known for its vast array of performances, from theater and comedy to dance, music, and experimental art, the Fringe draws millions of visitors and artists from around the globe. It is a celebration of creativity, diversity, and artistic expression in its purest form.

When and Where

The Edinburgh Festival Fringe takes place annually in August, typically running for three weeks from early to late in the month. The festival spans across multiple venues in the city, with performances happening in theaters, churches, bars, and even outdoor spaces throughout central Edinburgh.

What to Expect

The Edinburgh Festival Fringe is all about embracing diversity in the arts. You can expect an incredible variety of performances, from mainstream theater to avant-garde productions, stand-up comedy, cabaret, circus acts, street performances, and experimental works. The festival is known for being open-access, meaning anyone can perform, and there are thousands of shows to choose from.

The atmosphere is electric, with the streets filled with street performers, musicians, and people handing out flyers to promote their shows. You'll find a mix of well-established acts and up-and-coming talent, creating an exciting and dynamic environment where creativity knows no bounds.

Expect to see performances in every genre imaginable, including:

- Theater: Classic plays, contemporary pieces, and experimental performances.

- Comedy: Stand-up, sketch shows, and improv comedy from global and local talent.

- Dance and Physical Theater: Contemporary and classical dance performances, alongside unique physical theater acts.

- Music: Live concerts ranging from classical ensembles to indie bands, jazz, folk, and more.

- Cabaret and Burlesque: Sizzling performances that push boundaries in both entertainment and art.

- Children's Shows: Family-friendly performances that cater to younger audiences with plenty of fun and education.

What to Explore in Edinburgh During the Fringe

- Royal Mile: This iconic street is the heart of Edinburgh's Old Town and comes alive during the Fringe. Street performers, buskers, and costumed actors line the Mile, offering impromptu shows and performances.

- Edinburgh Castle: While attending the festival, don't miss exploring Edinburgh's most famous landmark. Perched atop Castle Rock, it offers incredible views and rich history.

- Holyrood Palace: Visit the official residence of the British monarch in Scotland, a short walk from the Royal Mile.

- Arthur's Seat: Take a hike up this extinct volcano for panoramic views of the city and surrounding landscapes.

- National Museum of Scotland: Explore Scotland's history, art, and culture in one of Edinburgh's most celebrated museums.

How to Get There

- By Air: Edinburgh Airport (EDI) is well-connected to major cities in the UK and internationally, making it easy to fly in for the festival. From the airport, you can take a tram, bus, or taxi to the city center.

- By Train: Edinburgh Waverley Station is the main railway station in the city, with frequent services connecting Edinburgh to other parts of Scotland and England.

- By Bus: National bus services (e.g., Megabus, National Express) provide affordable options for traveling to Edinburgh from various UK cities.

- By Car: If driving, there are numerous car parks in and around Edinburgh's city center. Keep in mind that parking can be limited during the festival, so public transport is often a better option.

- By Foot: Once you're in the city, Edinburgh is highly walkable, and many of the venues are within walking distance of each other, especially around the Old Town.

Cost of Attending the Fringe

The Edinburgh Festival Fringe is known for its accessibility, with ticket prices varying widely depending on the type of performance and venue.

- Show Tickets: Tickets for performances generally range from £5 to £20, though you'll find some shows with entry by donation or low-cost tickets for earlier performances. Special events or larger productions at major venues may have higher prices.

- Free Performances: Many street performers and outdoor shows are free, with the opportunity to donate or tip the performers if you enjoyed the show.

- Accommodation: Prices can vary greatly, depending on the type of accommodation you choose. Budget options such as hostels and guesthouses range from £30–£80 per night, while mid-range hotels and private rentals range from £100–£200 per night during festival time. Luxury hotels can be £200+ per night.

- Food and Drinks: Edinburgh has a wide variety of dining options, from budget-friendly cafes and food stalls (around £5–£10 for a meal) to more upscale dining at restaurants (around £20–£40 per person). Many food stalls and cafes also offer vegetarian and vegan options.

- Transport: Public transport in Edinburgh, including buses and trams, is affordable, with single fares typically around £1.80 to £2.50. You can also purchase day passes for unlimited travel.

The Edinburgh Festival Fringe is a celebration of creativity, diversity, and artistic expression, offering something for everyone. Whether you're a theater lover, comedy fan, or simply looking to explore one of the world's most vibrant cultural events, the Fringe promises to deliver an unforgettable experience in the heart of Scotland's capital.

Hogmanay: Scotland's Legendary New Year's Eve Celebration

Hogmanay is the Scottish celebration of New Year's Eve, a vibrant and deeply rooted tradition that spans the entire country but reaches its peak in Edinburgh. Known for its incredible festivities, live music, parades, and fireworks, Hogmanay is a night of revelry, marking the end of one year and the beginning of another with unique customs and an infectious sense of joy.

When and Where

Hogmanay takes place every year on December 31st, as Scotland celebrates the turn of the year in grand style. While the event is celebrated across the country, the biggest and most famous festivities happen in Edinburgh, where the streets come alive with music, dancing, and revelry.

What to Expect

Hogmanay is all about a communal celebration, and you can expect to experience the following:

- Torchlight Procession: The festivities begin on December 30th with the Torchlight Procession. Thousands of people walk through the streets of Edinburgh holding torches, marching to the sound of bagpipes and drums. The procession ends with a spectacular fireworks display.

- Street Parties and Live Music: On New Year's Eve, the streets of Edinburgh are transformed into massive outdoor venues, with multiple stages hosting live bands, DJs, and performers. From pop music to traditional Scottish tunes, the city fills with the sounds of celebration.

- Traditional Scottish Music and Dance: You'll find ceilidh dancing (traditional Scottish folk dancing) at many of the events, where both locals and visitors come together to dance to live folk bands. The infectious rhythm and high-energy steps of the ceilidh are one of the festival's main attractions.

- Fireworks and Midnight Countdown: As midnight approaches, the city's skyline is illuminated by breathtaking fireworks that light up the sky over Edinburgh Castle. The famous midnight countdown is accompanied by the singing of "Auld Lang Syne," a Scottish anthem that brings everyone together to ring in the New Year.

- First Footing: A beloved Scottish tradition, First Footing involves being the first person to enter a friend's or family member's home after midnight. Traditionally, this "first footer" brings a gift, such as a lump of coal (symbolizing warmth and prosperity) or whisky, to ensure good luck for the coming year.

What to Explore in Edinburgh During Hogmanay

•	Edinburgh Castle: The iconic castle sits proudly above the city and is a focal point of the Hogmanay celebrations, offering incredible views of the fireworks and surrounding festivities.

•	The Royal Mile: This historic street becomes a hub of activity during Hogmanay, with street performers, market stalls, and live music adding to the excitement.

•	Calton Hill: For a more peaceful vantage point, head to Calton Hill, where you can enjoy panoramic views of Edinburgh and the surrounding areas, including the fireworks display.

•	Holyrood Palace: The Palace of Holyroodhouse, located at the foot of the Royal Mile, is a beautiful spot to visit before the night's festivities begin. The surrounding parkland is peaceful and offers stunning views of the city.

•	Princes Street Gardens: During Hogmanay, Princes Street Gardens often host special events, including open-air concerts, and provide an excellent spot to relax or enjoy a hot drink while taking in the festivities.

How to Get There

•	By Air: Edinburgh Airport (EDI) is the main international gateway to the city. From the airport, you can take a bus, tram, or taxi to the city center. The city's well-connected transport network makes it easy to reach the celebrations.

•	By Train: Edinburgh Waverley Station is located in the heart of the city and is accessible via regular trains from cities across Scotland and the UK.

•	By Bus: Long-distance buses (e.g., Megabus, National Express) connect Edinburgh with other cities. Within the city, buses are a convenient way to get around, especially if you're heading to or from the celebrations.

•	By Car: While driving to Edinburgh is an option, the city center can get crowded during Hogmanay, and parking can be challenging. Public transport or walking is often the most convenient way to navigate during the festivities.

•	Walking: Once in the city, Edinburgh is very walkable, and many of the Hogmanay events are within walking distance of each other, especially around the Royal Mile and Princes Street.

Cost of Attending Hogmanay

•	Event Tickets: Access to some of the key events, such as the street party, live music performances, and the fireworks display, requires purchasing tickets. Ticket prices can range from £20 to £70, depending on the event and proximity to the main stage.

•	Accommodation: Prices for accommodation in Edinburgh can be higher during Hogmanay due to the popularity of the event. Budget options such as hostels and guesthouses can cost from £50–£100 per night, while mid-range hotels and private rentals range from £100–£200. Luxury hotels can cost upwards of £200 per night.

- Food and Drinks: There are plenty of food stalls and temporary bars during Hogmanay. Expect to pay around £5–£10 for street food and snacks. Drinks in the city's pubs and bars typically range from £4 to £8 for a pint or cocktail, with prices rising in festival zones.

- Public Transport: Public transportation is relatively affordable. Single fares for buses and trams within the city are around £1.80 to £2.50, and you can also purchase day passes for unlimited travel.

Hogmanay is one of the most spectacular celebrations of the year in Scotland. Whether you're dancing the night away, watching the incredible fireworks, or soaking in the rich traditions, it's an unforgettable way to welcome the new year. Edinburgh's Hogmanay celebrations offer an energetic and joyful atmosphere that will leave you with memories of a lifetime.

Highland Games: A Celebration of Scottish Tradition and Strength

The Highland Games are one of Scotland's most cherished traditions, drawing both locals and visitors for a combination of athletic competition, cultural performances, and fun. These games, which have been celebrated for centuries, showcase the strength, endurance, and spirit of Scottish heritage. With events taking place throughout the country, the Highland Games provide a thrilling glimpse into Scotland's past and present.

When and Where

The Highland Games typically occur during the summer months, from May to September, with the peak season being in July and August. These events are held across Scotland, particularly in rural villages, towns, and the picturesque Scottish Highlands. Some of the most popular Highland Games events include:

- Braemar Gathering: Held in Braemar, Aberdeenshire, this is one of Scotland's most prestigious Highland Games events, often attended by members of the Royal Family.

- Cowal Highland Gathering: This event in Dunoon, on the west coast of Scotland, is the largest of its kind and features the best of Scottish athleticism, music, and dance.

- Inverness Highland Games: Held in Inverness, the capital of the Scottish Highlands, this event offers a combination of traditional athletic events and modern-day competitions.

- Perth Highland Games: One of the older Highland Games, this event in Perth features a mix of traditional sports, cultural activities, and live entertainment.

What to Expect

The Highland Games offer a unique blend of athletic feats, cultural experiences, and traditional festivities. Visitors can expect the following:

- Traditional Athletic Events:

  - Caber Toss: This iconic event involves throwing a tall wooden log (caber) end over end. The athlete must toss the caber so that it lands in a specific position, with the small end touching the ground.

- - Tug of War: Teams of competitors engage in a strength contest to pull a heavy rope in opposite directions.
  - Hammer Throw: Athletes throw a heavy weight (resembling a hammer) attached to a handle as far as they can.
  - Stone Put: Similar to shot put, athletes throw a large stone as far as possible.
  - Weight for Height: Competitors toss a heavy weight over a bar set at a high level using only one hand.
  - Track and Field Events: These may include sprints, relay races, and other athletic competitions.
- Cultural Performances:
  - Pipe Bands: Bagpipe bands provide live music, filling the air with traditional Scottish tunes that energize the crowd.
  - Highland Dancing: Colorful performances of traditional Scottish dance, featuring intricate footwork and vibrant costumes, are a popular part of the games.
  - Celtic Music: In addition to bagpipes, traditional folk musicians perform lively Scottish tunes, adding to the festive atmosphere.
  - Scottish Clans: Many Highland Games celebrate Scottish clan history, where representatives from different clans wear their traditional tartans and provide information about their clan heritage.
- Other Highlights:
  - Parades: Some Highland Games feature parades showcasing the athletes, musicians, and local dignitaries.
  - Food and Drink: Traditional Scottish food like haggis, shortbread, and Scotch whisky are commonly available at food stalls.

What to Explore During the Highland Games

Beyond the excitement of the Highland Games, there is plenty to explore in the surrounding areas:

- Scenic Landscapes: Many of the games are held in the heart of the Scottish Highlands, where visitors can enjoy breathtaking views of mountains, valleys, and lochs.
- Historic Castles: Explore iconic Scottish castles like Braemar Castle and Inverness Castle, which are often located near Highland Games venues.
- Cairngorms National Park: If you're in the Braemar area, Cairngorms National Park offers spectacular landscapes and a chance to experience the beauty of the Highlands.

- Loch Ness: While in Inverness for the games, take the opportunity to visit Loch Ness, famous for its legendary monster, Nessie.

How to Get There

- By Air: The main international airports are Edinburgh and Glasgow. From there, you can take a train, bus, or drive to the Highland Games venues. Inverness also has an airport if you are heading specifically to that region.

- By Train: Scotland has an extensive train network, and many Highland Games locations are accessible by train. The journey from Edinburgh or Glasgow to Inverness or other Highland towns offers scenic views.

- By Bus: Many bus companies, including Citylink, offer services to towns and villages where the Highland Games are held.

- By Car: Renting a car is a good option if you wish to explore more rural parts of Scotland or attend several Highland Games in different locations. Make sure to check road conditions in the Highlands, especially in more remote areas.

- By Foot: Many games are set in scenic locations, and if you're nearby, walking and hiking around these events can add to the experience.

Cost of Attending the Highland Games

- Tickets: The cost of admission varies depending on the event. For example, general admission to major games like the Braemar Gathering may cost between £20 and £30, while smaller events might charge £10–£15.

- Accommodation: Accommodation prices in areas hosting the games range from budget options like hostels (£30–£60 per night) to mid-range hotels (£80–£150 per night) and more luxurious stays (£200+ per night).

- Food and Drink: Expect to pay £5–£15 for meals at the food stalls, with drinks (such as a pint of beer or Scotch whisky) ranging from £3–£7.

- Transportation: Public transport to Highland Games sites can cost between £10 and £50, depending on your starting point. If you choose to rent a car, prices vary, with daily rental rates typically starting from £30–£50.

The Highland Games are a spectacular celebration of Scotland's strength, culture, and history. Whether you are watching athletes compete in traditional events, enjoying the music and dance performances, or simply soaking in the local culture, attending a Highland Games event offers a memorable experience. With its unique blend of athleticism, tradition, and Scottish pride, the Highland Games are truly an unmissable part of Scottish life.

The Royal Edinburgh Military Tattoo: A Spectacular Celebration of Music and Tradition

The Royal Edinburgh Military Tattoo is one of Scotland's most iconic events, showcasing a unique blend of military precision, stunning performances, and captivating music. Held annually as part of the Edinburgh Festival, the Tattoo attracts visitors from all over the world, offering a spectacular experience that celebrates Scottish heritage and the global influence of the armed forces.

When and Where

•   When: The Royal Edinburgh Military Tattoo takes place every August during the Edinburgh Festival. It usually runs for about three weeks, starting in early August and concluding at the end of the month.

•   Where: The Tattoo is held at Edinburgh Castle, perched atop Castle Rock in the heart of Edinburgh. The stunning backdrop of the ancient fortress, with its sweeping views of the city, enhances the grandeur of the event.

What to Expect

The Royal Edinburgh Military Tattoo is a celebration of military music, precision marching, and cultural performances. Here's what you can expect:

•   Military Bands and Marching: The Tattoo brings together military bands from around the world. Performers showcase their musical talents with precision drills and elaborate formations. Expect to see regimental bands, pipes and drums, and military music from countries including Scotland, Australia, Canada, the United States, and more.

•   Cultural Performances: Alongside the military bands, the Tattoo features performances of traditional Scottish dance, such as Highland dancing and the ever-popular Scottish reels. The blend of cultural music and dance creates a vibrant and energetic atmosphere.

•   International Participants: The event is renowned for its global participation, with bands and performers from various countries, all united under the theme of military excellence. Each performance reflects the culture and traditions of the countries involved, offering an eclectic mix of musical styles and interpretations.

•   Torchlight Processions: The Tattoo features mesmerizing torchlight processions, where performers march through the grounds of Edinburgh Castle with flaming torches. This creates a dramatic and awe-inspiring visual spectacle.

•   The Massed Pipes and Drums: One of the most iconic moments of the Tattoo is the grand finale, where hundreds of bagpipers and drummers come together to perform in perfect harmony, creating a thunderous and electrifying sound that echoes through the castle and the surrounding city.

What to Explore During the Tattoo

While attending the Royal Edinburgh Military Tattoo, there is plenty to explore in and around Edinburgh:

- Edinburgh Castle: The Tattoo is set against the stunning backdrop of Edinburgh Castle, which is a must-visit historic site. Explore the castle's ancient walls, the Crown Jewels of Scotland, and the Stone of Destiny.

- The Royal Mile: Edinburgh's iconic street that stretches from the castle to the Palace of Holyroodhouse is lined with shops, restaurants, and historic sites, offering a taste of Scottish culture and history.

- Holyrood Palace: At the end of the Royal Mile is the Palace of Holyroodhouse, the official residence of the British monarch in Scotland. It's a must-see for history enthusiasts and those interested in royal life.

- Arthur's Seat: For panoramic views of the city, hike up Arthur's Seat, an extinct volcano that offers breathtaking vistas of Edinburgh and its surroundings.

- Edinburgh Old and New Towns: Explore the UNESCO-listed Old and New Towns, with their cobbled streets, hidden alleys, and charming squares that are full of history, art, and culture.

How to Get There

- By Air: Edinburgh is easily accessible by air, with Edinburgh Airport being the main international gateway. From the airport, you can take a tram or bus to the city center, which is about a 25-minute journey.

- By Train: Edinburgh is well-connected by rail, and trains to Edinburgh Waverley Station arrive from all major cities in the UK. From the station, the Royal Edinburgh Military Tattoo venue, Edinburgh Castle, is just a short walk away.

- By Bus: Several bus services operate throughout Scotland, including from Glasgow and other major cities. National Express and Citylink offer regular services to Edinburgh.

- By Car: Edinburgh is easily accessible by car, with excellent road links to the rest of Scotland and the UK. If driving, there are several car parks around the city, but parking near the castle can be limited during the Tattoo.

- On Foot: The Tattoo venue is centrally located in Edinburgh, and walking is one of the best ways to explore the city, especially when it comes to the Royal Mile and the nearby attractions.

Cost of Attending the Royal Edinburgh Military Tattoo

The cost of attending the Royal Edinburgh Military Tattoo varies depending on the seat location and the time of booking:

- Tickets: Prices for tickets generally range from £30 to £120. The more expensive tickets tend to be closer to the action, offering a better view of the performances. You can choose from a variety of seating options, including stand tickets, seats with a view of the castle, and VIP tickets for an enhanced experience.

- Accommodation: Edinburgh sees an influx of visitors during the Tattoo, so accommodation can be pricier during this time. Budget options like hostels start at around £30–£50 per night, while mid-range hotels typically cost £80–£150 per night. Luxury hotels can exceed £200–£300 per night.

- Food and Drink: Expect to pay around £5–£10 for snacks and drinks at the venue, while restaurants in the city center offer meals ranging from £10–£30 per person.

- Transportation: Public transportation within Edinburgh is affordable, with single bus or tram rides costing around £1.80–£2.50. A day pass for unlimited travel on buses and trams is available for about £4–£5. If taking a taxi, expect to pay around £10–£20 for a short ride.

The Royal Edinburgh Military Tattoo is a dazzling display of music, precision, and tradition, set against the stunning backdrop of Edinburgh Castle. With a captivating blend of military bands, cultural performances, and the mesmerizing sound of bagpipes, this event offers a once-in-a-lifetime experience for visitors. Whether you are a music lover, history enthusiast, or simply looking to experience the spirit of Scotland, the Tattoo is an unmissable event on the Edinburgh calendar.

Isle of Skye Music Festival: A Harmonious Celebration of Music and Scenic Beauty

The Isle of Skye Music Festival is a vibrant celebration of live music set on the stunning Isle of Skye, located off the west coast of Scotland. Known for its breathtaking landscapes, the festival combines the natural beauty of the island with a diverse range of musical genres, from traditional Scottish tunes to contemporary performances. It's an event that draws music lovers, nature enthusiasts, and those seeking a unique cultural experience.

When and Where

- When: The Isle of Skye Music Festival typically takes place every year in May, marking the beginning of the island's summer season. The festival usually spans over a long weekend, providing ample time to enjoy the music, explore the island, and immerse yourself in the festivities.

- Where: The festival is hosted in Portree, the largest town on the Isle of Skye. The primary festival site is often the Portree's Aros Centre or outdoor stages set in picturesque locations around the island, including the stunning coastal areas, making it an ideal venue to enjoy both the music and the surrounding natural beauty.

What to Expect

The Isle of Skye Music Festival is known for its eclectic lineup of musical performances, combined with the unique charm of the island. Here's what you can expect:

- A Diverse Range of Music: The festival offers something for everyone, featuring a mix of genres such as traditional Scottish folk, rock, indie, jazz, blues, and world music. Local Scottish musicians share the stage with international artists, creating a diverse musical landscape.

- Local Talent: The festival highlights the incredible talent that the Isle of Skye and Scotland have to offer. Expect to hear traditional Scottish music with bagpipes, fiddles, and accordions, alongside contemporary genres like folk rock and electronic music.

- Stunning Locations: Concerts are often set against the backdrop of Skye's dramatic landscapes. Imagine listening to live performances with the soaring peaks of the Cuillin Mountains in the distance or overlooking the beautiful Loch Portree. The setting itself adds to the magic of the event.

- Workshops and Masterclasses: In addition to live performances, the festival also offers workshops and masterclasses for aspiring musicians. These sessions provide attendees with the opportunity to learn from professional musicians, explore new instruments, and engage with the local music community.

- Community Spirit: The Isle of Skye Music Festival is known for its welcoming and inclusive atmosphere. The island's small, tight-knit community comes together to celebrate music and share their local culture with festival-goers, fostering a warm and friendly environment.

What to Explore During the Festival

While attending the Isle of Skye Music Festival, take time to explore the island's incredible landscapes and attractions:

- Portree: The charming capital of the Isle of Skye, Portree offers a scenic harbor, colorful buildings, and local shops where you can buy Scottish goods and souvenirs. Enjoy traditional Scottish cuisine, including fresh seafood and local specialties.

- The Old Man of Storr: A must-see geological feature, the Old Man of Storr is a rocky outcrop that has become one of Skye's most iconic landmarks. Hiking up to this stunning location offers magnificent views of the island.

- Fairy Pools: Located near the Cuillin Mountains, the Fairy Pools are crystal-clear, turquoise pools fed by waterfalls, perfect for a scenic hike or a peaceful swim during warmer weather.

- Dunvegan Castle: Explore the historic Dunvegan Castle, the oldest continuously inhabited castle in Scotland, home to the MacLeod clan for over 800 years. The castle grounds and gardens are also beautiful to explore.

- Neist Point Lighthouse: A visit to Neist Point on Skye's western tip offers breathtaking coastal views and the chance to see the iconic lighthouse perched on the cliff.

How to Get There

- By Air: The nearest major airport is Inverness Airport, located about a 3-hour drive from the Isle of Skye. From Inverness, you can take a bus or drive to Skye. Alternatively, there is a small airport on the island at Broadford, but flights are limited.

- By Train: The closest train station to the Isle of Skye is Kyle of Lochalsh, which is a 30-minute drive from the island. Trains run from Glasgow and Inverness to Kyle of Lochalsh. From there, you can take a bus or drive to Portree.

- By Car: Driving to the Isle of Skye offers a scenic route through the Scottish Highlands. From the mainland, cross the Skye Bridge, or take a ferry from Mallaig to Armadale on Skye's southern tip.

- By Bus: Several coach services operate from Glasgow, Edinburgh, and Inverness to the Isle of Skye. The bus ride provides picturesque views as you travel through the Highlands.

Cost of Attending the Isle of Skye Music Festival

The Isle of Skye Music Festival offers an affordable experience for those attending:

- Tickets: Day tickets typically range from £20 to £50, depending on the performances and the length of the festival. Weekend passes or VIP tickets, which may include access to exclusive events and workshops, can range from £80 to £150.

- Accommodation: Accommodation prices on the Isle of Skye can vary. Budget options like hostels and guesthouses start at £30–£60 per night, while mid-range hotels and bed-and-breakfasts can cost between £70–£120 per night. During the festival, booking early is essential to secure a place to stay.

- Food and Drink: Local eateries offer hearty meals such as fish and chips, haggis, and freshly prepared seafood, with prices typically ranging from £10 to £30 per person. Festival food stalls will also offer quick snacks and beverages.

- Transportation: If traveling by bus, single fares range from £15 to £30 from cities like Inverness to Skye. For those driving, expect to pay for fuel and parking, especially during peak festival time. Car hire on the island can be around £30–£50 per day.

- Other Activities: If you plan on exploring Skye's attractions, many of the island's natural wonders, such as hiking routes and scenic viewpoints, are free to access. Entrance to Dunvegan Castle is around £10 per adult, and other attractions may have similar entry fees.

The Isle of Skye Music Festival is a fantastic way to experience the stunning landscapes of one of Scotland's most beautiful islands, all while enjoying a diverse range of live music performances. Whether you're a music aficionado, a lover of natural beauty, or someone seeking a vibrant cultural experience, the Isle of Skye Music Festival offers a truly unique blend of entertainment and exploration. This festival is perfect for those looking to immerse themselves in both the music scene and the scenic splendor of Scotland's western coast.

Let me know if you need further details or additional assistance!

Chapter 4: Outdoor Adventures in Scotland

Hiking in the Highlands and National Parks

Highlands Hiking: Cairngorms National Park and Lochaber

Scotland's Highlands offer some of the most breathtaking and challenging hiking trails in the world, with a variety of terrains from rugged mountains to serene glens. Below are detailed descriptions of two of the most popular hiking regions in the Scottish Highlands: Cairngorms National Park and Lochaber.

Cairngorms National Park

Description: Cairngorms National Park, located in the heart of the Scottish Highlands, is the largest national park in Scotland and the UK. The park covers over 1,700 square miles and features a spectacular range of landscapes, from towering mountain peaks to vast forests and crystal-clear lochs. This region is home to the Cairngorm Mountains, which boast some of the highest peaks in the UK, including Ben Macdui, the second-highest mountain in Scotland. The park is a haven for wildlife enthusiasts, with species such as red squirrels, golden eagles, and wildcats calling it home.

Level:

- Easy to Advanced: The Cairngorms offer a wide range of hiking options, from easy walks along the shores of lochs to challenging mountain ascents. Routes like Glenmore Forest are suitable for beginners, while the more advanced hikes, such as those leading to Ben Macdui, require good fitness and experience in mountain walking.

What to Expect:

- Stunning Views: The park is known for its dramatic views, from sweeping valleys to the rugged peaks of the Cairngorm Mountains.

- Diverse Wildlife: Keep an eye out for rare species, including red deer, ptarmigans, and golden eagles. The area is also renowned for its excellent birdwatching opportunities.

- Varied Terrain: Expect to hike through a variety of terrains, including ancient forests, wild moorlands, and rocky mountain paths.

- Weather Conditions: The weather can change rapidly in the Cairngorms, especially at higher altitudes. Expect cooler temperatures and potential rain, particularly in the autumn and winter months.

What to Explore:

- Loch an Eilein: A picturesque loch surrounded by forests, perfect for a peaceful walk or a picnic.

- Ben Macdui: For experienced hikers, summiting Ben Macdui offers spectacular views of the surrounding mountains and valleys.

- Rothiemurchus Estate: This area offers a variety of walking routes, wildlife watching, and the opportunity to experience the park's ancient Caledonian pine forests.

- Glenmore Forest Park: An excellent starting point for many trails, with options ranging from short walks to more challenging hikes.

How to Get There:

- By Car: The Cairngorms National Park is accessible by car from cities like Inverness (about 40 miles away) or Aberdeen (about 80 miles away). The park is well-connected by a network of scenic roads, with plenty of parking near trailheads.

- By Train: You can take a train to Aviemore, one of the main towns in the Cairngorms. Aviemore is well-connected by train from Inverness and Edinburgh.

- By Bus: Local buses from Inverness and other nearby towns will take you into key areas of the park, including Aviemore and Grantown-on-Spey.

Cost:

- Free Entry: There is no charge to enter Cairngorms National Park, but some specific attractions, such as guided wildlife tours or indoor attractions like the Cairngorm Reindeer Centre, may have an entry fee of around £5 to £10.

- Accommodation: Camping is free in most areas, but there are also numerous campsites and accommodation options ranging from budget-friendly hostels (£15–£25 per night) to more luxurious hotels (£70–£120 per night).

- Transport: If traveling by train, a round-trip from Inverness to Aviemore can cost around £15–£30, depending on the time of year and booking method.

Lochaber

Description: Lochaber, located in the western Scottish Highlands, is a rugged and diverse region known as the "Outdoor Capital of the UK." It is home to Ben Nevis, the highest mountain in the British Isles, as well as other notable peaks like Aonach Mor and Glen Nevis. The area is famous for its steep, dramatic landscapes, which include deep valleys, lochs, and coastal cliffs. Lochaber offers an exceptional range of hikes, catering to beginners, intermediate hikers, and seasoned mountain climbers.

Level:

- Easy to Advanced: Lochaber has something for every level. The lowland trails around the Glen Nevis area are suitable for beginners, while more challenging climbs like Ben Nevis require advanced skills and preparation.

What to Expect:

- Mountain Challenges: The park's highlight is Ben Nevis, which attracts hikers from around the world. Expect steep, rocky climbs, especially near the summit of Ben Nevis, where you will be rewarded with panoramic views over the Highlands.

- Scenic Beauty: The area is full of breathtaking scenery, from tranquil lochs such as Loch Linnhe to the expansive glens and towering mountain peaks.

- Variable Weather: The weather in Lochaber can be unpredictable, especially in the mountains, so always prepare for rain, cold temperatures, and sudden weather changes.

What to Explore:

- Ben Nevis: The most famous hike in Lochaber, summiting Ben Nevis is an essential challenge for any keen hiker. The Mountain Track (also known as the Pony Track) is the most popular route, though it is demanding and requires good fitness.

- Glen Nevis: For less challenging hikes, explore Glen Nevis, with its stunning waterfalls, rivers, and views of Ben Nevis. A great spot for easier trails and beautiful scenery.

- Aonach Mor: The second-highest peak in Lochaber, Aonach Mor offers exhilarating hikes and a ski resort during the winter. It can be accessed via a gondola ride, providing a unique perspective of the region.

- Loch Linnhe: Enjoy a peaceful walk along this scenic loch, with stunning views of the surrounding mountains.

How to Get There:

- By Car: Lochaber is easily accessible by car, with Fort William serving as a central hub. It's about a 1.5-hour drive from Inverness and 3.5 hours from Glasgow.

- By Train: The town of Fort William is well-served by train, with routes from Glasgow and Mallaig.

- By Bus: There are several bus services to Fort William from major cities like Glasgow and Inverness. The town is also connected by coach services to surrounding areas.

Cost:

- Free Entry: Hiking in Lochaber, including Ben Nevis, is free of charge. However, some guided tours or specific mountain activities (like skiing) may incur fees.

- Accommodation: There are budget hostels (£20–£30 per night) and more luxurious options in Fort William (£70–£150 per night). Camping is available at many sites around Lochaber.

- Transport: A train from Glasgow to Fort William costs around £20–£40 one-way, depending on time and booking. Bus tickets are usually £10–£20.

Both Cairngorms National Park and Lochaber offer unique hiking experiences, from the rugged mountain trails of the Cairngorms to the iconic challenge of summiting Ben Nevis in Lochaber. Whether you're an experienced mountaineer or a beginner looking for scenic walks, these regions in the Scottish Highlands provide unparalleled outdoor adventures amidst some of the most spectacular landscapes in the UK.

National Parks Hiking: Cairngorms National Park and Loch Lomond & The Trossachs National Park

Scotland's national parks are not only perfect for hiking but also showcase the country's diverse landscapes, from rugged mountains to serene lochs. Below is a detailed guide to two of Scotland's most renowned national parks: Cairngorms National Park and Loch Lomond & The Trossachs National Park.

Cairngorms National Park

Description: Cairngorms National Park, located in the heart of the Scottish Highlands, is the largest national park in Scotland and the UK. It spans more than 1,700 square miles and includes some of the highest mountains in Scotland, such as Ben Macdui, as well as ancient Caledonian forests and tranquil lochs. The park is home to a variety of wildlife, including red squirrels, golden eagles, and red deer, making it an excellent destination for nature lovers. The Cairngorms are known for their dramatic beauty and offer a wide range of hiking opportunities, from short forest walks to challenging mountain climbs.

Level:

- Easy to Advanced: Cairngorms National Park has trails for all levels. The lowland routes, such as those near Glenmore Forest, are perfect for beginners, while mountain trails, such as those to Ben Macdui, are more suited for experienced hikers.

What to Expect:

- Diverse Landscapes: Expect to explore rugged mountains, vast moorlands, lush forests, and pristine lochs. The varied terrain offers something for every hiker.

- Wildlife: The park is home to a variety of wildlife, including red deer, Scottish wildcats, and rare birds of prey like golden eagles.

- Scenic Views: Expect incredible panoramic views of the surrounding peaks, valleys, and forests.

- Variable Weather: Weather can change rapidly, especially at higher altitudes. Be prepared for rain, chilly winds, and possibly snow in winter months.

What to Explore:

- Ben Macdui: A challenging yet rewarding hike, Ben Macdui is Scotland's second-highest mountain. Reaching the summit offers panoramic views over the Cairngorms.

- Loch an Eilein: A picturesque, forested loch with a ruined castle on an island. This is an easier, more relaxed walk ideal for families or beginner hikers.

- Rothiemurchus Estate: Known for its ancient Caledonian pine forests, this estate offers a range of trails, including short walks and more extensive hikes.

- Glenmore Forest Park: A popular area for all types of hiking, with paths suitable for families and adventurers alike.

How to Get There:

- By Car: Cairngorms National Park is easily accessible by car from Inverness (about 40 miles) or Aberdeen (around 80 miles). The park is well-connected by scenic roads.

- By Train: Take a train to Aviemore, one of the park's key towns, which is well-served by trains from Inverness and Edinburgh.

- By Bus: Local buses from nearby towns such as Inverness and Aviemore connect you to key hiking areas within the park.

Cost:

- Free Entry: Entry to the park is free. However, specific attractions like guided tours, the Cairngorm Reindeer Centre, and some visitor centres may charge an entry fee (around £5–£10).

- Accommodation: Campsites are free in many areas, though you can find hostels (£15–£25 per night) or hotels (£70–£120 per night) in towns like Aviemore.

- Transport: Train tickets from Inverness to Aviemore typically range from £15–£30 for a return journey. Bus services are also available at similar prices.

Loch Lomond & The Trossachs National Park

Description: Loch Lomond & The Trossachs National Park, located in central Scotland, is one of the country's most popular parks. It covers over 720 square miles and is home to Loch Lomond, the largest freshwater lake in Scotland, surrounded by a beautiful mix of mountains, forests, and lochs. The park's landscape varies from rolling hills and dense woodlands to dramatic peaks and wild moorlands, offering a wide range of hiking opportunities. It's a perfect spot for those who enjoy not only hiking but also water-based activities, including canoeing and boating.

Level:

Easy to Advanced: Loch Lomond & The Trossachs has hikes suitable for all levels, from simple lakeside walks to demanding mountain climbs like Ben Lomond, the park's highest peak.

What to Expect:

- Waterfront Views: Expect scenic views of Loch Lomond, as well as several other beautiful lochs like Loch Katrine and Loch Awe.

- Woodland Trails: The park is rich in forests, providing serene walking paths surrounded by ancient trees, including oak and pine.

- Mountain Views: The park's rugged hills and peaks provide plenty of opportunities for hiking, with dramatic panoramas over the lochs and surrounding countryside.

- Wildlife: Expect to see a variety of wildlife, including red deer, ospreys, and a range of bird species.

What to Explore:

- Ben Lomond: The park's highest mountain, Ben Lomond, is a popular hike for experienced hikers, offering spectacular views over Loch Lomond and the surrounding area.

- Loch Katrine: Ideal for gentle walks, Loch Katrine is surrounded by beautiful woodlands. You can walk or cycle along the shore or take a boat ride for a different perspective.

- The Trossachs: A picturesque area filled with scenic woodlands, lochs, and glens. There are several trails of varying difficulty, offering a peaceful experience in nature.

- The West Highland Way: While primarily a long-distance trail, sections of this route pass through the southern part of the park, providing stunning views of Loch Lomond and the surrounding hills.

How to Get There:

- By Car: Loch Lomond & The Trossachs National Park is easily accessible by car from Glasgow (about 25 miles) or Stirling (around 20 miles). The park is well-served by roads with access to key walking areas.

- By Train: The towns of Balloch and Alexandria are easily reached by train from Glasgow, and both provide convenient access to the southern part of the park.

- By Bus: Regular bus services run from Glasgow to various parts of the park, including Callander, Aberfoyle, and Balloch.

Cost:

- Free Entry: Entry to the park is free. However, certain attractions like Loch Katrine may charge for boat trips (around £10–£20).

- Accommodation: Camping is available in designated areas, and there are hostels (£15–£25 per night) and hotels (£70–£150 per night) in the nearby towns.

- Transport: A round-trip train from Glasgow to Balloch typically costs £8–£15. Bus tickets range from £5–£10 depending on the distance and route.

Both Cairngorms National Park and Loch Lomond & The Trossachs National Park offer incredible opportunities for hiking, with landscapes ranging from high mountain peaks to peaceful lochs and forests. Whether you're after a challenging climb or a scenic lakeside walk, these parks have something for every hiker, along with plenty of options for exploring the surrounding natural beauty.

Loch Ness and Boat Tours

Loch Ness is one of Scotland's most famous and enchanting destinations, attracting visitors from around the world for its deep, mysterious waters, beautiful landscapes, and, of course, the legendary Loch Ness Monster, affectionately known as Nessie. Located in the Scottish Highlands, near the town of Inverness, Loch Ness is not only steeped in myth and folklore but also offers a wealth of activities for those who enjoy nature, history, and adventure. One of the best ways to experience the loch's natural beauty is through a boat tour, providing visitors with stunning views of the surrounding hills, castles, and villages.

Description of Loch Ness

Loch Ness is a large freshwater lake stretching about 23 miles (37 kilometers) in length and reaching depths of up to 754 feet (229 meters), making it one of the deepest lochs in Scotland. Surrounded by rugged landscapes, forests, and the majestic Great Glen, Loch Ness offers a combination of mystery, tranquility, and breathtaking scenery. The loch is famous for its long-standing legends about the Loch Ness Monster, though the area also boasts a rich history, including ancient ruins, castles, and scenic walking paths along its shores.

What to Expect at Loch Ness

- Stunning Scenery: From the calm waters of the loch to the rolling hills and ancient woodlands that surround it, Loch Ness is a place of incredible natural beauty. As you take a boat tour, you'll be treated to panoramic views of the Highland landscape, with sweeping vistas that change as you make your way along the loch.

- Historical Landmarks: There are several castles and ancient ruins around Loch Ness. The most famous is Urquhart Castle, a stunning medieval fortress that overlooks the loch. The castle is steeped in history and offers dramatic views of the water, especially from a boat on the loch.

- The Loch Ness Monster: While sightings of Nessie are rare, many visitors hope to catch a glimpse of the elusive creature. The area is filled with quirky "monster" themed shops and attractions, adding a touch of fun to the experience.

- Calm Waters: Depending on the weather, Loch Ness offers relatively calm waters, making it a peaceful and relaxing destination for a boat tour. The boat rides are typically smooth, allowing you to take in the breathtaking views without disturbance.

What to Explore Around Loch Ness

- Urquhart Castle: One of the most popular historic sites around Loch Ness, Urquhart Castle is a must-see. Visitors can explore its ruins, including the Great Hall, the Grant Tower, and lochside walkways, offering fantastic views of Loch Ness. From the boat, you can also see the castle from a unique perspective on the water.

- Inverness: The nearby city of Inverness, about a 30-minute drive from Loch Ness, offers shops, restaurants, and historical sites. It's a great place to stop and explore after visiting the loch.

- Fort Augustus: This charming village sits at the southern tip of Loch Ness and is home to the famous Caledonian Canal. You can watch the locks in action or take a boat tour on the canal. It's a great place for lunch or a stroll along the water.

- The Loch Ness Centre & Exhibition: Located in Drumnadrochit, this interactive museum offers an in-depth look at the history and mystery of Loch Ness, including scientific explanations and local folklore. It's an educational and fun stop for those curious about the loch's history and the Nessie legend.

Boat Tours on Loch Ness

A boat tour is one of the best ways to experience Loch Ness, allowing you to soak in the beauty of the loch and its surrounding landscapes. Various companies offer boat tours ranging from short trips to longer, more extensive excursions.

What to Expect on a Boat Tour:

- Guided Tours: Most boat tours are guided, and the guides provide informative commentary on the history, geography, and legends of Loch Ness. You'll learn about the Nessie sightings, the ancient castles, and the surrounding landscape.

- Views of the Loch: As you glide across the water, you'll have incredible views of the surrounding hills and forests, which look especially stunning when bathed in the golden light of sunrise or sunset.

- Potential for Wildlife Sightings: Although sightings of Nessie are rare, you may spot a variety of other wildlife, including birds, otters, and even the occasional deer grazing along the shore.

Types of Boat Tours:

- Short Tours: Short boat trips typically last around 1 to 1.5 hours, offering views of the loch, Urquhart Castle, and nearby landmarks. These are perfect for those with limited time but still want to experience the beauty of Loch Ness from the water.

- Extended Tours: Longer tours can last up to 2–3 hours and may include stops at nearby attractions such as Urquhart Castle. These tours provide a more in-depth experience of the loch and its surrounding area.

- Private Charters: If you prefer a more personalized experience, many companies offer private boat charters, allowing you to explore the loch at your own pace with a dedicated guide.

- Kayaking and Canoeing: For a more adventurous experience, visitors can rent kayaks or canoes to explore the loch at a slower pace. This gives you an opportunity to get closer to the water and enjoy the serene atmosphere.

How to Get There

- By Car: Loch Ness is easily accessible from Inverness (approximately 20 miles), which is connected by major roads such as the A82. It is a scenic drive that offers great views of the loch.

- By Bus: Regular buses run from Inverness to the villages around Loch Ness, including Drumnadrochit and Fort Augustus, making it easy to reach the loch from the city.

- By Train: Inverness is well-connected by train to major Scottish cities, including Edinburgh and Glasgow. From Inverness, buses or taxis can take you to Loch Ness.

Cost

- Boat Tours: The cost of a boat tour on Loch Ness can range from £15–£25 for a short trip to £30–£50 for a longer or private tour. Some boat companies also offer family tickets or group discounts.

- Urquhart Castle: Entry to Urquhart Castle is priced around £9.50–£12.00 for adults, with discounts available for children and seniors.

- Other Costs: If you plan to visit nearby attractions or participate in activities like kayaking, expect additional costs. For example, canoe rentals can be around £20–£30 for a few hours.

Loch Ness is not only a place of natural beauty but also rich in history and folklore. Whether you're interested in exploring the mysterious waters, enjoying a relaxing boat ride, or discovering historic castles, there is something for everyone around Loch Ness. Boat tours are one of the best ways to experience the loch, offering unique views of the surrounding landscape and a chance to explore the area from a different perspective.

Isle of Skye's Fairy Pools

The Fairy Pools on the Isle of Skye are one of Scotland's most enchanting natural wonders, located at the foot of the Black Cuillin Mountains. These crystal-clear, spring-fed pools are famous for their stunning beauty, and they offer visitors an opportunity to experience the magic and tranquility of one of Scotland's most picturesque landscapes. Whether you're looking to enjoy a peaceful walk, take stunning photographs, or even dip your toes into the refreshing waters, the Fairy Pools have something to offer.

Description of the Fairy Pools

The Fairy Pools are a series of freshwater pools and waterfalls located near the village of Glenbrittle on the Isle of Skye. The pools are known for their clear, turquoise water, which is fed by the nearby Allt Coir' a' Mhadaidh stream, which flows down from the Black Cuillin Mountains. The pools are surrounded by rugged mountain terrain, grassy hillsides, and dramatic rock formations, making them an ideal place for nature lovers and outdoor enthusiasts.

What to Expect at the Fairy Pools

•   Breathtaking Scenery: The Fairy Pools are set in a dramatic landscape, with jagged mountain peaks rising in the background and lush greenery surrounding the pools. The crystal-clear water is set against dark rocks and grassy banks, creating a picturesque scene that seems almost otherworldly.

•   Peaceful Atmosphere: Despite being a popular tourist destination, the Fairy Pools are surprisingly peaceful, especially in the early morning or later in the evening. The sound of water flowing over rocks and the sight of cascading waterfalls make it an ideal place for relaxation and reflection.

•   Swimming and Dipping: While the water can be cold, some visitors choose to take a quick dip in the pools. The crystal-clear water is refreshing, and the experience of swimming or wading in the pools surrounded by mountains is truly magical. However, be prepared for a brisk, invigorating swim due to the low temperatures.

•   Waterfalls and Streams: The pools are connected by a series of small waterfalls that cascade down from the mountains, adding to the beauty of the area. These waterfalls create a soothing sound and provide ample opportunities for photography.

What to Explore Around the Fairy Pools

•   Black Cuillin Mountains: The Fairy Pools are located at the base of the Black Cuillin Mountains, one of Scotland's most rugged and dramatic mountain ranges. If you're an experienced hiker, you can explore the nearby trails that lead up into the mountains, offering incredible views of the pools and surrounding landscape.

- Glenbrittle Beach: A short drive from the Fairy Pools is Glenbrittle Beach, where you can enjoy a peaceful stroll along the shore. The beach offers sweeping views of the coastline and the Isle of Rum in the distance.

- Dunvegan Castle: Located further along the Isle of Skye, Dunvegan Castle is home to the Clan MacLeod and is a historic landmark worth exploring. The castle is surrounded by lush gardens and offers beautiful views of the surrounding area.

- The Old Man of Storr: While not immediately next to the Fairy Pools, The Old Man of Storr is another must-see landmark on the Isle of Skye. It's one of the island's most iconic geological formations and offers a challenging but rewarding hike to the top.

What to Expect from a Visit

- Accessible Walk: The Fairy Pools are accessible via a well-marked walking path from the car park at Glenbrittle. The walk to the pools is relatively easy, with a duration of around 30 minutes to an hour, depending on your pace and how often you stop to take in the views. The path is gravelly in places, so sturdy footwear is recommended.

- Ideal for Photographers: The Fairy Pools offer a perfect setting for photography, with their striking landscapes and dramatic lighting. Whether you're capturing the waterfalls, the pools, or the surrounding mountains, this spot offers plenty of opportunities for stunning shots.

- Wildlife Spotting: While the Fairy Pools are mainly known for their beauty, they're also home to a variety of local wildlife. Birdwatchers may spot species such as golden eagles, ravens, and kestrels soaring above the mountains. Otters and other small animals may also be spotted in the surrounding areas.

How to Get There

- By Car: The Fairy Pools are located about 18 miles (29 kilometers) from Portree, the main town on the Isle of Skye, along the A87 road. The drive takes approximately 30 minutes. Once you reach Glenbrittle, you'll find a car park where you can leave your vehicle and begin your walk to the pools.

- By Public Transport: Public transport to the Fairy Pools can be limited, as the Isle of Skye is a rural area. However, buses do run from Portree to Glenbrittle, and you can check schedules ahead of time. Once in Glenbrittle, the walk to the Fairy Pools is short and easy to navigate.

- By Taxi: If you're staying in Portree or another nearby area, you may choose to take a taxi to the Fairy Pools. This is a good option if you're not keen on driving, though it may be more expensive.

Cost

- Parking: There is a small parking fee at the Glenbrittle Car Park, which is around £5 for the day. This fee helps maintain the facilities and trails around the Fairy Pools.

- Free Admission: Access to the Fairy Pools is free, so there are no entry fees. However, it's important to respect the natural environment and avoid disturbing the wildlife.

- Optional Costs: If you choose to take a guided tour or participate in activities like wildlife watching, there may be additional costs. Some tour companies offer packages that include transportation and guided walks around the Isle of Skye, which typically range from £40–£80 per person, depending on the duration and services included.

The Fairy Pools on the Isle of Skye are a breathtaking and magical destination, offering visitors an opportunity to experience the beauty and tranquility of the Scottish Highlands. With their crystal-clear water, stunning waterfalls, and surrounding landscapes, the Fairy Pools are a must-see for nature lovers, photographers, and outdoor enthusiasts. Whether you're taking a leisurely walk, swimming in the refreshing water, or simply soaking in the scenery, a visit to the Fairy Pools will leave you with unforgettable memories of one of Scotland's most enchanting natural wonders.

Cycling and Biking Routes in Scotland

Scotland offers a vast network of scenic cycling and biking routes that take you through its dramatic landscapes, from rugged mountain ranges to tranquil lochs and beautiful coastal areas. Whether you're a casual rider or an experienced cyclist, Scotland has something to offer every level of rider, making it one of the best places in the world to enjoy cycling in nature.

Description of Cycling in Scotland

Scotland's diverse geography makes it an ideal destination for cyclists of all kinds. The country boasts a variety of terrains—from smooth, flat roads that wind through picturesque villages to rugged, off-road trails through mountainous terrain. Cycling here is not just about getting from one place to another; it's about experiencing the stunning landscapes, wildlife, and rich history that Scotland has to offer. The National Cycle Network (NCN) connects major cities and towns, and there are countless routes that cater to road cyclists, mountain bikers, and leisure riders alike.

What to Expect When Cycling in Scotland

- Diverse Terrain: From the flat, scenic roads of the Scottish Lowlands to the rugged off-road trails of the Highlands, the terrain in Scotland is as diverse as it gets. Expect to cycle through ancient forests, beside sparkling lochs, and up steep mountain passes, each offering unique challenges and rewards.

- Breathtaking Views: Scotland is known for its dramatic landscapes, and cycling allows you to experience them in an up-close and personal way. Whether it's the rolling hills of the Trossachs, the rugged peaks of the Cairngorms, or the serene coastlines of Loch Ness, each route offers breathtaking views.

- Wildlife Sightings: Cycling through Scotland's rural areas and national parks offers plenty of opportunities to spot local wildlife. Deer, red squirrels, otters, and birds of prey are common in the Highlands and forests. Keep your eyes peeled for these magnificent creatures as you ride through Scotland's natural beauty.

- Accessible for All: Scotland is home to a range of cycling routes suitable for all levels. From smooth paths through urban areas to more challenging mountain routes, there's something for every rider. Whether you're a beginner looking for an easy route or an experienced rider ready to conquer tough trails, you'll find a ride that suits your skill level.

Popular Cycling Routes to Explore

- North Coast 500 (NC500): A stunning 500-mile (800 km) route along the Scottish Highlands that offers cyclists an unforgettable adventure. The route starts and ends at Inverness and takes riders through the northernmost point of Scotland, offering panoramic views of coastal cliffs, rugged mountains, and beautiful beaches.

- The Great Glen Way: This route follows the famous Great Glen from Inverness to Fort William, running parallel to Loch Ness. It's perfect for cyclists looking for a scenic route with a mix of terrain, including forest paths, loch-side trails, and mountain passes. The total distance is around 73 miles (117 km), making it suitable for cyclists of all levels.

- The Hebridean Way: This long-distance cycling route runs through the Western Isles, connecting the Isle of Lewis in the north to The Isle of Barra in the south. It's an ideal route for those who enjoy coastal cycling with breathtaking views of the Atlantic Ocean, sandy beaches, and quiet roads. The full route spans 156 miles (252 km).

- Kintyre Way: This 100-mile (161 km) route along the Kintyre Peninsula takes you through quiet roads and coastal paths, offering views of rugged cliffs and rolling hills. This route is perfect for those who want to combine cycling with exploring some of Scotland's remote villages and natural beauty.

- The Borders Loop: This 130-mile (210 km) route loops through the Scottish Borders, taking cyclists on a journey through rolling hills, valleys, and charming towns like Peebles and Melrose. It's a great option for riders looking for a relatively flat route with stunning views of the countryside.

- Isle of Skye Cycling Routes: The Isle of Skye offers a variety of cycling routes, ranging from coastal paths to more challenging hill climbs. One popular route is the A87, which runs from Portree to Broadford, offering cyclists dramatic views of the Cuillin Mountains and the surrounding coastline.

- Loch Lomond & The Trossachs National Park: This national park offers cyclists an abundance of routes, including a scenic loop around Loch Lomond. The area offers a mix of road cycling and off-road tracks through forests and along loch sides, with plenty of chances to spot wildlife and enjoy stunning views of the Scottish countryside.

What to Explore Along the Cycling Routes

- Castles: Scotland is home to countless castles, many of which are located along cycling routes. Stop by Urquhart Castle on the shores of Loch Ness, or visit Stirling Castle after cycling through the surrounding countryside.

- Lochs: Cycling beside Scotland's lochs is one of the most scenic experiences. Routes like the Great Glen Way offer stunning views of Loch Ness and Loch Lochy, while Loch Lomond provides another stunning setting for cycling through the national park.

- Historical Sites: Many cycling routes take you past historical landmarks, including ancient battlefields, stone circles, and prehistoric sites. Take a break at Culloden Moor, the site of the famous Battle of Culloden, or explore the Neolithic village of Skara Brae on the Orkney Islands.

- Outdoor Adventures: For those interested in other outdoor activities, Scotland is a hub for hiking, climbing, and kayaking. Take advantage of your cycling route to explore nearby trails, or kayak on the serene waters of a loch.

- Villages and Towns: As you cycle through Scotland, you'll have the opportunity to stop in charming villages and towns, such as Pitlochry, Dornoch, and Oban. These areas are perfect for rest stops, offering local cuisine, cozy cafes, and beautiful historic architecture.

What to Expect on Your Cycling Journey

- Variable Terrain: Some routes will have smooth, tarmacked paths, while others will take you on rugged, uneven surfaces. Be prepared for both types of terrain, especially if you plan to tackle off-road trails or mountain biking routes.

- Challenging Climbs: Many of Scotland's cycling routes involve significant climbs, particularly in the Highlands and mountain areas. While the views from the top are incredible, riders should be prepared for some physically demanding ascents.

- Changeable Weather: Scotland's weather can be unpredictable, so it's essential to pack for all conditions. Rain showers and strong winds are common, so make sure to bring appropriate clothing, including waterproof gear, and check the weather forecast before heading out.

- Support and Facilities: Many popular cycling routes have designated bike shops, cafés, and rest stops along the way, particularly in more tourist-friendly areas like Edinburgh, Inverness, and Portree. These facilities offer bike repairs, food, and other essential services.

How to Get Around on Cycling Routes

- By Car: The best way to get to the start of many cycling routes is by car. Scotland's well-maintained roads provide easy access to most routes, and many routes have designated parking areas near the start points.

- By Train: Scotland has a reliable train system, and many train stations are located near popular cycling routes. Consider taking a train to Inverness, Fort William, or Edinburgh, where you can start your cycling adventure.

- By Bus: Some areas in Scotland, particularly the Highlands and islands, are served by bus routes that accommodate bicycles. Check with local bus companies for specific schedules and policies.

- By Bike Hire: If you don't have your own bike, you can easily rent one in many of Scotland's larger cities or near popular cycling routes. Many places offer mountain bikes, road bikes, or e-bikes to suit your needs.

Cost

- Bike Rental: The cost of renting a bike in Scotland can range from £20 to £40 per day, depending on the type of bike and location. Mountain bikes and electric bikes tend to be more expensive.

- Bike Hire Locations: Many bike hire shops also offer guided cycling tours, which can range from £30 to £100 per person, depending on the length and level of the tour.

- Transport Costs: Train and bus tickets vary by location, but a single train ride with your bike can cost around £10–£20. Bus services may charge an additional fee for carrying your bike.

- Accommodations: Many cycling routes offer a range of accommodation options, from budget hostels to luxury hotels. Budget around £50 to £100 per night for a mid-range hotel or guesthouse, with cheaper options available for hostels or campsites.

Cycling in Scotland is an incredible way to explore the country's diverse landscapes and enjoy its stunning natural beauty. From the coastal roads of the Hebrides to the rugged mountain paths of the Cairngorms, Scotland offers a wide range of cycling routes that cater to all levels of cyclists. Whether you're interested in leisurely rides through picturesque countryside or challenging climbs in the Highlands, Scotland provides an unforgettable cycling experience.

Whale Watching in the Hebrides

The Hebrides, an archipelago off the west coast of Scotland, is one of the most renowned spots for whale watching in the UK. With its rugged coastlines, deep waters, and abundant marine life, it offers the perfect environment for observing these majestic creatures in their natural habitat. Whether you're an experienced wildlife enthusiast or a first-time visitor, whale watching in the Hebrides is a thrilling experience that promises unforgettable sightings and stunning views.

Description of Whale Watching in the Hebrides

The Hebrides are located along the Inner and Outer Hebrides, a series of islands with dramatic coastal landscapes and nutrient-rich waters. This region provides the perfect habitat for several whale species, including the majestic minke whale, the playful bottlenose dolphins, and the occasional killer whale. The waters around the Hebrides are also home to numerous other marine mammals and birds, making it a popular destination for wildlife enthusiasts.

The warm waters of the Atlantic Ocean meet the cold waters of the North Sea here, creating an ideal environment for feeding whales, particularly during the summer months when plankton and small fish abound. The Hebrides have become an increasingly popular location for whale watching tours, with several experienced tour operators offering specialized trips.

What to Expect

- Minke Whales: The minke whale is the most commonly spotted whale in the Hebrides. These whales are usually around 7-10 meters long and are easily recognizable by their sleek, dark bodies. Minke whales are often seen during the summer months as they feed in the rich waters of the Hebrides.

- Orca (Killer Whales): The waters around the Hebrides are occasionally visited by the powerful killer whale. While sightings are rarer than those of the minke whale, orcas have been spotted in these waters, especially around the islands of Skye, Islay, and the Outer Hebrides.

- Humpback Whales: Humpback whales are also known to migrate through the Hebrides, often seen breaching and tail-slapping in the open ocean. These sightings are less common but still spectacular when they occur.

- Other Marine Life: In addition to whales, the Hebrides are teeming with other fascinating marine life. Dolphins, especially bottlenose dolphins and common dolphins, are often spotted performing acrobatic leaps near the boats. Seals, porpoises, and even the occasional sea otter can also be seen during a tour. The waters around the islands are also home to a wide variety of seabirds, including puffins, gannets, and eagles.

- Scenic Views: Whale watching in the Hebrides is not just about the wildlife; it's also about the stunning scenery. The islands are surrounded by pristine, crystal-clear waters, and the boat trips offer panoramic views of rugged coastlines, towering cliffs, and rolling hills. On clear days, the snow-capped peaks of the Cairngorms and Ben Nevis can even be seen in the distance.

What to Explore Around Whale Watching

- Islands to Visit: Several islands in the Hebrides are well-known for their whale-watching opportunities. Isle of Skye, Islay, Mull, and the Outer Hebrides are particularly popular, each offering a unique perspective of the ocean and abundant wildlife.

- The Isle of Skye: Skye is not only renowned for its whale-watching opportunities but also for its breathtaking landscapes, including the Old Man of Storr, Fairy Pools, and the Cuillin Mountains. The island has several reputable tour operators that can guide you to the best whale-watching spots.

- Mull and the Sound of Mull: The Sound of Mull is one of the best places in the Hebrides to spot minke whales and other marine life. The island of Mull also has historical sites, including Duart Castle and Tobermory, a picturesque town that offers plenty of opportunities for sightseeing and exploration after a day of whale watching.

- The Outer Hebrides: These islands, which include Lewis, Harris, and Barra, are known for their remote beauty and exceptional wildlife. The Sound of Harris is particularly famous for its orca sightings, and the islands' isolated nature offers a chance to experience a peaceful, untouched wilderness.

How to Get There

- By Ferry: The Hebrides are accessible by ferry from mainland Scotland. Several ferry companies operate routes from Oban, Ullapool, and Mallaig to various islands in the Hebrides. Once on the islands, whale-watching tours are usually a short drive or walk from the ferry terminals.

- By Car: Hiring a car is the best way to explore the Hebrides at your own pace. Roads are generally well-maintained, although some areas may be remote and require a bit of adventure. Car rentals are available at airports and ferry terminals on the mainland.

- By Plane: There are also flights available to several islands, including Isle of Skye, Islay, and Harris, with regular services from Glasgow and Edinburgh. Flying is a convenient option if you're short on time.

When to Go

The best time to go whale watching in the Hebrides is during the summer months, from May to September. This is when the whale activity is at its peak, as minke whales and other species come to the area to feed. Early summer (June and July) offers the best chance of seeing humpback whales and orcas, while the latter part of summer (August and September) is ideal for spotting minke whales and dolphins.

Cost

- Whale Watching Tours: Whale-watching tours in the Hebrides typically cost around £30 to £60 per person for a half-day trip. Full-day tours or private charters can be more expensive, ranging from £80 to £150 or more, depending on the duration and type of boat.

- Accommodation: The cost of accommodation in the Hebrides varies widely depending on the season and location. Budget options like hostels and campsites can start from around £25 per night, while mid-range guesthouses and B&Bs typically charge £60 to £100 per night. Luxury hotels and self-catering cottages can cost £100+ per night.

- Ferries: Ferry tickets to the Hebrides are reasonably priced, with round-trip fares ranging from £20 to £50 depending on the island and the time of year. Cars are usually an additional fee, with charges ranging from £20 to £40 for a car and passengers.

Whale watching in the Hebrides is an awe-inspiring experience that allows you to connect with the natural world in a way few other activities can. Whether you're out on a boat in search of the powerful orca, marveling at the graceful minke whale, or simply enjoying the beauty of Scotland's rugged coastline, the Hebrides offer some of the best whale-watching opportunities in Europe. With its remote charm, rich wildlife, and spectacular views, a whale-watching trip in the Hebrides is sure to be one of the most memorable adventures of your life.

Chapter 5: Cultural and Historical Attractions

Edinburgh Castle and the Royal Mile

Edinburgh Castle, perched atop the extinct volcano Castle Rock, is one of the most iconic landmarks in Scotland. Dominating the city's skyline, the castle has a rich history that spans over a thousand years. Its strategic location and stunning views of the surrounding city make it a must-visit destination for anyone exploring Edinburgh. Situated along the Royal Mile, a historic street that connects the Castle to the Palace of Holyroodhouse, the castle is at the heart of the city's history, culture, and tradition.

Edinburgh Castle: What to Expect

- Historic Significance: Edinburgh Castle has been a royal residence, a military stronghold, and a symbol of Scottish power throughout its history. It has witnessed countless battles, royal ceremonies, and historic events. The castle has housed Scottish kings and queens, including Mary, Queen of Scots, and has played a crucial role during times of conflict, such as the Wars of Scottish Independence.

- Key Attractions:

  o The Crown Jewels: The Crown Jewels of Scotland, including the Stone of Destiny, which was used for the coronation of Scottish kings, are housed in St. Margaret's Chapel within the castle. Visitors can marvel at the intricate craftsmanship and the historical significance of these royal symbols.

  o St. Margaret's Chapel: This tiny, serene chapel is the oldest surviving building in Edinburgh, dating back to the 12th century. It stands as a peaceful testament to the city's long history.

  o The Great Hall: The Great Hall is one of the castle's largest rooms, used for royal ceremonies and banquets. Its massive wooden beams and impressive armor displays transport visitors to medieval Scotland.

  o The National War Museum of Scotland: Situated inside the castle, this museum offers an extensive collection of military artifacts that tell the story of Scotland's military history.

  o The One O'Clock Gun: Every day, except Sundays, the One O'Clock Gun is fired from the castle's ramparts, a tradition that dates back to 1861. Visitors can experience this historic moment, which still serves as a time signal for the city.

  o The Crown and the Scottish Royal Arms: Visitors can view the Scottish Crown and other regalia used in the coronation of Scottish monarchs.

What to Explore Around Edinburgh Castle

- The Royal Mile: The Royal Mile is a historic thoroughfare that runs from the Edinburgh Castle at the top of the hill down to the Palace of Holyroodhouse. It is lined with centuries-old buildings, shops, restaurants, and historical sites. Walking the Royal Mile is an immersion in Edinburgh's past, with highlights including:

- St. Giles' Cathedral: A stunning example of Gothic architecture, St. Giles' is Edinburgh's most famous cathedral, known for its crown-like spire and rich religious history.

- The Real Mary King's Close: Hidden beneath the city, this is a fascinating tour of underground streets and rooms that have remained preserved since the 17th century.

- The Scottish Parliament Building: At the foot of the Royal Mile, the Parliament building is an example of modern architecture and the center of Scottish political life.

- Museum of Edinburgh: Located on the Royal Mile, this museum offers a detailed look into Edinburgh's past, from medieval times to modern-day.

- Grassmarket: A vibrant area just below the castle, the Grassmarket offers a lively atmosphere with pubs, restaurants, and shops. The historic square has been a hub of trade, entertainment, and even executions over the centuries.

- Princes Street Gardens: A beautiful park in the heart of Edinburgh, just a short walk from the castle, these gardens offer serene walks, impressive floral displays, and views of the castle from the lower levels.

What to Expect

When you visit Edinburgh Castle, expect a blend of awe-inspiring history, breathtaking views, and fascinating exhibitions. The castle's grand architecture and the panoramic views of the city and surrounding hills are sure to leave a lasting impression. Visitors will experience a combination of interactive exhibits, well-preserved historical rooms, and stunning outdoor areas that provide insights into Scotland's past.

The Royal Mile will transport you through time as you stroll past cobbled streets, medieval alleys (known as closes), and traditional Scottish shops. The area is always bustling with street performers, tourists, and locals, making it a vibrant, energetic part of the city. The Royal Mile is also home to a wide variety of shops selling Scottish souvenirs, tartans, kilts, and traditional Scottish food.

How to Get There

- By Foot: Edinburgh Castle is centrally located in Edinburgh, and can easily be reached on foot from most places within the city. It sits atop Castle Hill, just off the Royal Mile. A short walk from Waverley Station or the Bus Station will bring you directly to the castle.

- By Bus: Numerous buses travel through High Street and the Royal Mile, with the nearest stops being close to Grassmarket and St. Giles' Cathedral. The Lothian Buses are an excellent and convenient way to get around the city.

- By Taxi: You can also take a taxi directly to the entrance of the castle if you prefer a more comfortable or direct route.

Cost

- Edinburgh Castle Admission: The cost of admission to Edinburgh Castle is approximately £18 for adults, with discounted rates for children, students, and seniors. Entry is free for children under 5 years old.

- Royal Mile: Access to the Royal Mile is free, and you can walk it at your leisure. However, individual attractions along the Royal Mile, such as the Real Mary King's Close or St. Giles' Cathedral, may have entry fees of around £10-£15.

- Royal Edinburgh Ticket: If you plan on visiting multiple attractions like Edinburgh Castle, Holyrood Palace, and The Royal Yacht Britannia, consider purchasing the Royal Edinburgh Ticket. This pass offers discounted entry to several major Edinburgh attractions and is valid for 48 hours.

- Guided Tours: Guided walking tours along the Royal Mile or of the castle can cost between £15 and £25 per person. These tours often include expert insight into the history of the site and the city.

A visit to Edinburgh Castle and the Royal Mile is an essential part of any trip to the Scottish capital. From the breathtaking views at the castle to the rich history woven into every stone of the Royal Mile, these landmarks offer a perfect introduction to Edinburgh's fascinating past. Whether you're exploring the castle's ancient rooms, strolling down cobbled streets lined with history, or enjoying a traditional Scottish meal along the way, Edinburgh's rich heritage and vibrant culture are on full display.

Urquhart Castle and Loch Ness

Nestled on the shores of the iconic Loch Ness, Urquhart Castle is a historic ruin that stands as a symbol of Scotland's medieval past. With its dramatic location overlooking the shimmering waters of Loch Ness and surrounded by lush landscapes, the castle offers visitors a glimpse into the rich history and mystique of the region. Often associated with the legendary Loch Ness Monster, Urquhart Castle is a must-see destination for history buffs, nature lovers, and those eager to explore the myth and magic of this famous loch.

Urquhart Castle: What to Expect

- Historic Significance: Urquhart Castle dates back to the 13th century and has witnessed many significant events in Scotland's history. Originally built to defend the Great Glen, the castle was heavily involved in the wars between the Scots and the English. It has been a site of numerous sieges and battles, often changing hands between the Scots and the English, and has ties to Scottish kings and battles for independence.

- Key Attractions:

  o The Ruins: The castle's ruins are a powerful testament to Scotland's medieval military past. The Great Hall, Lord's Tower, and Gatehouse are among the most recognizable parts of the castle, each offering unique insight into the structure's history.

  o The Grant Tower: The tower provides stunning panoramic views of Loch Ness and the surrounding area. It's a great spot for photos and to appreciate the castle's strategic location.

- Exhibition Centre: The on-site exhibition center is home to a variety of displays and artifacts that offer a deeper understanding of Urquhart Castle's role in Scottish history. Interactive exhibits and multimedia presentations bring the castle's past to life.

- Loch Ness Views: From Urquhart Castle, visitors can enjoy breathtaking views over the Loch Ness waters. The location provides a perfect vantage point to explore the region and imagine the battles that once took place on the land.

- Loch Ness Monster: As one of the most famous legends in Scotland, Loch Ness is known worldwide for the Nessie sightings. While at Urquhart Castle, visitors can also explore the mystery surrounding the Loch Ness Monster.

What to Explore Around Urquhart Castle and Loch Ness

- Loch Ness: Beyond the castle, Loch Ness itself is a focal point for visitors. Known for its deep waters and mysterious reputation, Loch Ness offers plenty to explore:

- Boat Tours: Visitors can take boat tours around Loch Ness, some of which include stops at key sites along the loch, such as Castle Urquhart. The boat tours offer a unique perspective of the castle and its scenic surroundings.

- Loch Ness Centre & Exhibition: Located in Drumnadrochit, this center is dedicated to the history, geography, and the legend of the Loch Ness Monster. It provides an in-depth look at the local environment, wildlife, and scientific exploration of the loch.

- Walking Trails: There are several walking trails around Loch Ness, offering both easy strolls and more challenging hikes. These trails offer the chance to enjoy the beautiful scenery and nature of the Scottish Highlands.

- Drumnadrochit Village: A short distance from Urquhart Castle, Drumnadrochit is a charming village that is home to a variety of shops, restaurants, and Nessie-themed attractions.

What to Expect

When you visit Urquhart Castle and Loch Ness, expect a mix of historical intrigue, stunning views, and the opportunity to experience Scotland's natural beauty. The ruins of the castle are atmospheric and full of character, allowing you to imagine what life was like during medieval times. The location, sitting on the shores of the famously mysterious Loch Ness, adds an element of legend and folklore to the experience. The sound of the wind, the breathtaking scenery, and the occasional ripple of Loch Ness's deep waters combine to create a memorable atmosphere.

Visitors can also expect a chance to learn more about the mystery of the Loch Ness Monster, with information and exhibits that delve into the legend of "Nessie." Whether you're a history enthusiast, a nature lover, or a believer in the Loch Ness myth, this area offers something for everyone.

How to Get There

- By Car: Urquhart Castle is easily accessible by car, and there is a car park at the entrance to the site. It's located along the A82 road, about 21 miles (34 km) south-west of Inverness. The drive offers scenic views of the surrounding countryside, and the road leading to the castle is well-marked.

- By Bus: There are regular bus services from Inverness to Drumnadrochit, which is the closest village to Urquhart Castle. From there, visitors can take a short taxi ride or walk to the castle itself.

- By Boat: Visitors arriving by boat can take a Loch Ness Cruise which often includes a stop at Urquhart Castle. These cruises are a fun way to explore the loch from the water, with beautiful views of the castle along the way.

Cost

- Urquhart Castle Admission: Entry to Urquhart Castle is approximately £12.50 for adults, with discounts available for children, students, and seniors. Family tickets are also available for around £30.

- Loch Ness Boat Tours: A boat tour of Loch Ness typically costs around £15-£25 per person, depending on the length of the tour and whether it includes stops at Urquhart Castle or other sites along the loch.

- Loch Ness Centre & Exhibition: Admission to the Loch Ness Centre & Exhibition is approximately £9.50 for adults, with discounts for children and seniors.

- Parking: Parking is available at Urquhart Castle for a small fee, typically around £3-£5 for a full day.

A visit to Urquhart Castle and Loch Ness offers a unique blend of history, natural beauty, and mystery. The castle ruins, standing proud on the edge of Loch Ness, provide a fascinating glimpse into Scotland's medieval past, while the surrounding landscapes invite exploration of one of the most famous bodies of water in the world. Whether you're admiring the historical remnants of the castle, enjoying a boat trip on the loch, or diving into the myth of the Loch Ness Monster, a trip to Urquhart Castle and Loch Ness is an unforgettable Scottish adventure.

The Falkirk Wheel

The Falkirk Wheel is an impressive feat of engineering, blending innovation with the rich history of Scotland's waterways. It is the world's first and only rotating boat lift, connecting two major canals – the Union Canal and the Forth and Clyde Canal. Located in the town of Falkirk, the wheel stands as a unique symbol of Scotland's commitment to modern technology while preserving its industrial past. This attraction is a must-see for anyone interested in engineering marvels, Scottish history, and scenic landscapes.

What to Expect at The Falkirk Wheel

- Innovative Design: The Falkirk Wheel is an extraordinary piece of modern engineering. It stands 35 meters high and has a span of 35 meters in width. The wheel lifts boats 24 meters from one canal to another in a fully rotational motion, using hydraulic power. Visitors can watch as the wheel turns, seamlessly transferring boats between the two canals without the need for traditional locks.

- Boat Ride Experience: Visitors can take a boat trip on the Falkirk Wheel, where they can experience the lifting process firsthand. These boat trips offer a unique perspective of the wheel in action and allow passengers to appreciate the massive scale of the structure and the surrounding countryside.

- The Wheel and Visitor Centre: The Falkirk Wheel is home to an excellent visitor center, which offers educational exhibits and displays about the history of the wheel, its design, and the canal system in Scotland. Interactive exhibits and films give visitors insight into the wheel's construction and its importance in reconnecting the Scottish canals.

- Falkirk Wheel Park and Trails: The surrounding area offers walking and cycling paths, allowing visitors to explore the beautiful scenery along the canal. The park is perfect for a leisurely stroll or a relaxing day out, and there are many spots to enjoy a picnic while taking in the views of the wheel and the tranquil canal waters.

- Cafe and Souvenir Shop: The Wheelhouse Cafe offers a delightful place to enjoy refreshments with views of the wheel. There's also a souvenir shop where visitors can purchase unique items related to the Falkirk Wheel and Scotland's canal heritage.

What to Explore Around The Falkirk Wheel

- Forth and Clyde Canal: The Falkirk Wheel is a key part of the Forth and Clyde Canal system, which stretches across central Scotland. Visitors can explore the canal by boat or on foot, and there are various spots along the canal for scenic walks.

- Union Canal: The Union Canal, connected to the Falkirk Wheel, stretches from Falkirk to Edinburgh. The canal is perfect for walking, cycling, and boating, offering picturesque views and a peaceful environment.

- The Antonine Wall: A UNESCO World Heritage Site, the Antonine Wall was once the northernmost frontier of the Roman Empire. Sections of the wall can be explored near the Falkirk Wheel, offering a fascinating glimpse into Scotland's Roman past.

- Callendar House and Park: Located nearby, Callendar House is a historic mansion set in beautiful parkland. It houses a museum with exhibits on local history and is an ideal place to visit for those interested in Scotland's heritage and architecture.

What to Expect

Visitors to the Falkirk Wheel can expect a fascinating combination of history, engineering, and scenic beauty. The wheel itself is the star attraction, and seeing it in operation is an awe-inspiring experience. Expect to be amazed by the sheer scale and elegance of this rotating boat lift as it lifts and lowers boats between the canals. The surrounding parkland and canals provide plenty of opportunities for leisurely exploration, while the visitor center offers a chance to delve into the technical details of the wheel's design and construction.

The experience is both educational and entertaining, making it suitable for visitors of all ages. Whether you're an engineering enthusiast, a history buff, or someone simply looking to enjoy a day out in beautiful surroundings, the Falkirk Wheel is a unique destination that offers something for everyone.

How to Get There

•	By Car: The Falkirk Wheel is easily accessible by car and is located just off the M9 motorway, approximately 30 minutes from Edinburgh and Glasgow. There is a large free parking area at the wheel for visitors.

•	By Train: The nearest train station to the Falkirk Wheel is Falkirk High Station, which is about 2 miles away. From the station, visitors can take a bus or a taxi to the wheel.

•	By Bus: There are regular bus services that run to the Falkirk Wheel from Falkirk town center, making it easy for visitors relying on public transport.

•	By Boat: During the summer months, visitors can travel to the Falkirk Wheel by boat along the canal system, enjoying a scenic route that ends at the wheel.

Cost

•	Falkirk Wheel Admission: Entry to the visitor center and the surrounding parkland is free. However, there is a charge for the boat trip on the wheel. A standard boat trip costs around £12 per adult and £6 for children. Family tickets are available at a discounted rate.

•	Parking: Parking is free at the Falkirk Wheel, making it an affordable option for visitors traveling by car.

•	Boat Hire: For those wishing to explore the canals by boat, boat hire is available. Prices for hiring a boat vary depending on the type of boat and the duration of hire, with options starting from around £25 per hour for smaller boats.

A visit to the Falkirk Wheel is a truly unique experience that combines Scotland's rich history with cutting-edge engineering. Whether you're fascinated by the technical brilliance of the rotating boat lift or simply looking to enjoy the beautiful surroundings, the Falkirk Wheel offers an unforgettable day out. With plenty of nearby attractions to explore and a visitor center full of information, it's a must-visit for anyone interested in Scotland's industrial past, natural beauty, and innovative future.

Scottish National Gallery

The Scottish National Gallery is one of Scotland's most renowned cultural institutions, home to an extensive collection of fine art spanning centuries. Located in the heart of Edinburgh, the gallery boasts works by some of the world's greatest artists, including Van Gogh, Turner, Rembrandt, and Vermeer. It is a must-visit for art lovers, history enthusiasts, and those wanting to immerse themselves in Scotland's rich cultural heritage. The gallery's setting, housed in a stunning neoclassical building on the Mound, adds to its charm, making it a landmark that complements the beauty of Edinburgh's historic Old Town.

What to Expect at the Scottish National Gallery

•	Impressive Art Collection: The gallery houses an extraordinary collection of European paintings and sculpture, ranging from the Renaissance to the 19th century. Highlights include iconic works by Van

Gogh like The Sower, Turner's atmospheric landscapes, and Vermeer's serene domestic scenes. It's a true paradise for art lovers, with numerous masterpieces waiting to be admired.

•	Scotland's Art Heritage: The gallery showcases a rich array of works by Scottish artists, including pieces by Henry Raeburn and William McTaggart, providing insight into Scotland's artistic development. Visitors can explore both historical and contemporary Scottish art, learning about the country's artistic evolution through time.

•	Temporary Exhibitions: In addition to its permanent collection, the Scottish National Gallery regularly hosts temporary exhibitions, which feature works from other prestigious collections around the world. These exhibitions cover a wide range of artistic periods, themes, and movements, ensuring that there is always something new to discover.

•	Interactive Exhibits: The gallery is designed to engage visitors of all ages and backgrounds. The use of interactive displays, guided tours, and audio guides help visitors explore and understand the art in an enriching and accessible way.

•	The Scottish National Gallery and Its Architecture: The gallery's neoclassical architecture is a piece of art in itself. Designed by William Henry Playfair, the building features grand columns, intricate stonework, and beautifully proportioned rooms. Visitors can enjoy not only the art but also the architectural beauty of the space.

What to Explore Around the Scottish National Gallery

•	Princes Street Gardens: Just outside the gallery lies the Princes Street Gardens, an expansive green space that offers a tranquil escape in the heart of the city. The gardens provide stunning views of the Edinburgh Castle and are an ideal spot for a relaxing walk or picnic after a visit to the gallery.

•	Edinburgh Castle: Located a short walk from the gallery, the Edinburgh Castle is one of the city's most famous landmarks. Visitors can explore the fortress, which houses the Crown Jewels of Scotland and offers panoramic views of Edinburgh and beyond.

•	National Gallery of Modern Art: A short stroll or bus ride away, the National Gallery of Modern Art complements the Scottish National Gallery, focusing on works from the 20th and 21st centuries. The two galleries offer a comprehensive overview of Scotland's art scene.

•	Royal Scottish Academy: Situated beside the Scottish National Gallery, the Royal Scottish Academy hosts exhibitions and displays of contemporary art, contributing to Edinburgh's vibrant art scene.

What to Expect

Visitors can expect to step into a world of artistic wonder. The collection spans over 700 years of art history, with works that inspire, provoke, and fascinate. From quiet contemplation in front of a serene Rembrandt portrait to the awe of seeing Turner's seascapes, the gallery offers a deeply enriching experience. It's a place where both art enthusiasts and casual visitors can lose themselves in masterpieces.

The gallery's location in the center of Edinburgh means it's surrounded by the city's vibrant atmosphere. After immersing yourself in the world-class art collection, you can step out into Edinburgh's bustling streets, where history, culture, and scenic views await. The gallery is an accessible space, welcoming visitors of all backgrounds and interests.

How to Get There

•	By Foot: Located in Princes Street, the Scottish National Gallery is easily accessible on foot from many of Edinburgh's key attractions, including the Royal Mile and Edinburgh Castle. It's situated in the city's cultural heart, surrounded by landmarks and amenities.

•	By Public Transport: Edinburgh has an efficient public transport system. Visitors can take Lothian Buses to get close to the gallery, with several bus routes stopping at or near Princes Street. The Waverley Railway Station is also within walking distance, making it easy to access the gallery from other parts of the city.

•	By Car: If driving, the gallery is located centrally, and there are paid parking facilities nearby. However, parking in the city center can be limited, so it's often easier to take public transport or walk.

•	By Bicycle: For cycling enthusiasts, Edinburgh has a bike-share system that allows easy access to various parts of the city, including the gallery.

Cost

•	Admission: Entry to the Scottish National Gallery is free for the permanent collection, making it an affordable cultural experience for everyone. Some special exhibitions or events may have an entry fee, typically ranging from £5 to £15 depending on the exhibition.

•	Guided Tours: The gallery offers guided tours, which provide a deeper understanding of the art and its history. These tours may have a small additional charge, typically around £5-£10.

•	Special Exhibitions: Temporary exhibitions often have a charge for entry. Prices for these vary depending on the exhibition, but most range between £10 and £20 for adults, with discounts for children, students, and senior citizens.

•	Donations: While entry is free, the gallery welcomes donations to help support its work and collections. There are donation boxes around the gallery for visitors who wish to contribute.

The Scottish National Gallery is a treasure trove of art, culture, and history. Whether you're a passionate art lover, a first-time visitor, or simply looking for a moment of quiet reflection in the heart of Edinburgh, this gallery offers an exceptional experience. Its stunning collection, combined with its central location and welcoming atmosphere, makes it an essential stop on any visit to Edinburgh. With free entry to the permanent collection and a variety of exhibitions and events throughout the year, the gallery is a place that offers something for everyone.

Chapter 6: Unique Scottish Experiences

Ghost Tours in Edinburgh

Edinburgh is often considered one of the most haunted cities in Europe, and its cobbled streets, ancient alleyways, and centuries-old buildings are ripe for spooky tales and ghostly encounters. With a rich history of crime, plague, witch trials, and executions, it's no surprise that ghost tours have become a popular way to experience the darker side of the Scottish capital. Whether you're a believer in the supernatural or just looking for a thrilling adventure, Edinburgh's Ghost Tours offer an unforgettable experience that combines the city's fascinating history with chilling tales of the unexplained.

What to Expect on a Ghost Tour

- Storytelling and History: Most ghost tours are guided by expert storytellers who are well-versed in Edinburgh's eerie history. Expect to hear spine-tingling stories about the city's haunted locations, mysterious happenings, and legendary ghosts. These tours are not just about the supernatural; they delve into the historical events that have left behind lingering spirits, such as burial grounds, old prisons, and execution sites.

- Haunted Locations: Many tours take you through some of Edinburgh's most haunted spots, such as the Greyfriars Kirkyard, where the infamous McKenzie Poltergeist is said to roam, or the Edinburgh Vaults, a dark and atmospheric series of underground chambers beneath the city that are notorious for paranormal activity.

- Atmosphere: Ghost tours are designed to be immersive, with guides often dressing in period costumes to set the mood. The tours typically take place in the evening, with darkness adding to the eerie atmosphere. The dimly lit streets and cobbled paths create a spooky environment where every corner holds the possibility of an unsettling encounter.

- Paranormal Experiences: Some tours offer the opportunity to use ghost-hunting equipment such as EMF meters, spirit boxes, and infrared cameras. While these tools are not always scientifically proven, they add an extra layer of thrill to the experience, especially if you're hoping to encounter something unexplainable.

What to Explore During a Ghost Tour

- The Edinburgh Vaults: Beneath the South Bridge lie the eerie Edinburgh Vaults, dark and damp chambers that were once used for everything from workshops to storage, and later became home to criminals and the destitute. The vaults are infamous for their haunting atmosphere, and many ghost tours visit them, with reports of unusual sounds, cold spots, and ghostly apparitions.

- Greyfriars Kirkyard: This historic graveyard is home to Greyfriars Bobby, but it's also said to be haunted by the vengeful spirit of George Mackenzie, a notorious 17th-century lawyer. Visitors have reported chilling encounters with cold, oppressive air and unseen forces, particularly near the infamous Black Mausoleum.

- Mary King's Close: Located beneath the Royal Mile, Mary King's Close is an old, narrow street that has been sealed off for centuries. Once home to merchants and residents, the close was later abandoned during a plague outbreak, and many believe the spirits of those who died there still linger. It's one of the most popular spots for ghost tours, with many reports of shadowy figures and unexplained phenomena.

- The Royal Mile: This historic street, which runs through the heart of Edinburgh's Old Town, is filled with haunted locations, including old buildings and alleyways where grisly tales of murder, betrayal, and torture unfold. Many ghost tours pass through this area, allowing visitors to experience the spine-chilling atmosphere.

- Edinburgh Castle: While not always included in ghost tours, Edinburgh Castle is another haunted location where visitors often report eerie feelings and sightings. With its centuries-old history of battles, executions, and tragedies, it's no wonder many believe that the spirits of fallen soldiers and tortured prisoners still haunt the castle grounds.

What to Expect

On an Edinburgh ghost tour, you can expect to be entertained and terrified in equal measure. While the tours are designed to be thrilling and atmospheric, guides often weave in humor and historical context, making the experience both informative and spine-chilling. You'll walk through dark, narrow streets, hear blood-curdling tales, and maybe even feel a ghostly chill on your neck.

Many tours are designed for all levels of bravery, from family-friendly ghost walks to more terrifying late-night expeditions that delve into darker themes. Some tours might even include theatrical elements, such as actors playing historical figures or ghostly apparitions, further enhancing the eerie experience.

How to Get There

- By Foot: Most ghost tours start from the Royal Mile, the heart of Edinburgh's Old Town. It's easy to find your way to the departure points, and since many tours operate within the Old Town, walking is the best way to explore.

- By Public Transport: Edinburgh is well-connected by bus, and most ghost tours are easily accessible from public transport stops around the city. If you're traveling by train, Edinburgh Waverley Station is close to the Royal Mile, making it convenient to join a ghost tour from there.

- By Taxi: If you prefer a more direct route, taxis are readily available throughout Edinburgh, and you can take one to the departure point of your chosen ghost tour.

Cost of Ghost Tours

The cost of a ghost tour in Edinburgh typically ranges from £10 to £25 per person, depending on the tour length, the locations visited, and the level of excitement. Some premium tours that include more exclusive access to haunted sites or ghost-hunting equipment may cost more, while shorter walks or family-friendly tours may be more affordable.

- Standard Tours: Typically cost around £10 to £15 per person for a 1-2 hour walking tour.

- Premium Tours: Tours that include ghost-hunting equipment, special access to haunted locations, or exclusive experiences can range from £20 to £25 per person.

- Private Tours: For a more personalized experience, private ghost tours can be arranged, with prices generally starting at around £40 to £50 for a group of up to four people.

Edinburgh's ghost tours offer a unique way to explore the city's haunted history while taking in its stunning architecture and ancient streets. Whether you're a skeptic or a true believer, the combination of chilling tales, atmospheric locations, and rich history makes these tours a must for anyone looking to experience the supernatural side of Scotland's capital.

Exploring Viking Heritage in Orkney

Orkney, an archipelago off the northern coast of Scotland, is steeped in rich Viking history that has shaped its culture, landscape, and traditions. The islands were once a thriving Viking settlement and remain a treasure trove of archaeological sites and fascinating stories of Norse invaders and settlers. If you're a history enthusiast, particularly interested in Viking heritage, Orkney offers an incredible opportunity to step back in time and explore the remnants of these ancient civilizations.

What to Expect in Orkney's Viking Heritage

Orkney is home to some of the most important Viking archaeological sites in the world. Many of these sites remain well-preserved, providing a window into how the Vikings lived, worked, and interacted with the landscape and other cultures. You can expect to explore everything from ancient burial sites to settlement ruins, stone circles, and Norse artifacts that tell the stories of this fascinating period in history.

- Viking Artifacts: You'll encounter a range of artifacts, including tools, weapons, jewelry, and pottery, many of which have been uncovered from Viking settlements. These objects provide insight into the everyday lives of the Norse people.

- Norse Place Names and Language: The Viking influence on Orkney's place names is still very much alive today. Many local place names are derived from Old Norse, and the language still resonates in the dialects spoken by Orkney's residents. As you explore the islands, you'll encounter names that reveal the rich Viking heritage embedded in the land.

Key Viking Sites to Explore

Orkney is home to several remarkable sites where you can immerse yourself in its Viking past. These locations give visitors a chance to walk in the footsteps of the Norsemen and women who once called the islands home.

- Skara Brae: Often referred to as Scotland's Pompeii, Skara Brae is a UNESCO World Heritage site and one of the best-preserved prehistoric settlements in Europe. Though the site predates the Vikings, the surrounding area was inhabited by the Norse, and the discovery of Viking artifacts here provides a direct connection to the Viking era. Explore the stone houses, ancient tombs, and Neolithic structures that offer clues to the early Viking settlers.

- Orkney's Viking Trail: The Viking Trail is a well-marked route through the islands that leads visitors to some of the most significant Viking sites. Highlights include The Earl's Palace in Kirkwall, the Brough of Birsay, and Stromness—each with its unique connection to Viking history. The trail provides an accessible way to explore the heart of Orkney's Viking heritage, with ample information and interpretation along the way.

- The Brough of Birsay: A small tidal island, the Brough of Birsay is home to the ruins of a Viking settlement and Norse longhouses. Visitors can explore the remains of Viking houses and fortifications on the island, which was once a key Norse stronghold. The Brough offers spectacular views of the surrounding coastline and is accessible via a causeway at low tide.

- St. Magnus Cathedral: While this stunning cathedral in Kirkwall is a medieval Christian structure, its history is deeply intertwined with the Vikings. St. Magnus Cathedral was founded by Rory, the Viking Earl of Orkney, and dedicated to his cousin St. Magnus, who was martyred by another Viking leader. The cathedral stands as a testament to the Viking influence on the Christianization of Orkney.

- The Earl's Palace, Kirkwall: Built in the 17th century by the Viking earls, The Earl's Palace is a grand ruin that highlights Orkney's Viking past. The structure offers insight into the power held by the Viking earls and their influence over the islands.

- Viking Boat Burial Site at Westray: Westray is home to a remarkable Viking boat burial, where archaeologists have uncovered a Viking ship along with human remains and various grave goods. This burial site provides a rare glimpse into Viking burial practices and their reverence for the sea.

What to Expect

Exploring Orkney's Viking heritage is like stepping into a time capsule, where you can immerse yourself in the sights and sounds of the past. You'll find:

- Ancient Ruins: From Viking settlements to burial sites, Orkney's landscape is dotted with ruins that are steeped in history. Many sites are easily accessible and offer self-guided tours, though guided tours are also available to help you fully appreciate the history behind each location.

- Interpretation Centers: To deepen your understanding of the Viking past, Orkney has several interpretation centers that provide in-depth exhibits on the Viking age. The Orkney Museum in Kirkwall is an excellent place to begin your exploration, showcasing Viking artifacts, maps, and multimedia exhibits.

- Natural Beauty: While exploring the Viking sites, you'll also be treated to breathtaking scenery. Orkney's rugged coastline, rolling hills, and tranquil lochs offer a beautiful backdrop to the historical sites, making it an ideal destination for both history lovers and nature enthusiasts.

How to Get There

Orkney can be reached by:

- Ferry: Ferries regularly depart from Scrabster (near Thurso on the mainland) to Stromness and Kirkwall on Orkney's main islands. The ferry journey offers picturesque views of the coastline and takes approximately 1 to 1.5 hours.

- Flight: Orkney also has an airport with direct flights from Aberdeen, Edinburgh, and Glasgow. The flight time is typically under an hour, making it a quick and convenient option for reaching the islands.

- By Car: Once on Orkney, you can explore the islands by car. Renting a vehicle is the most convenient way to visit the many historical sites, though some areas may require a short walk or ferry ride.

Cost

- Ferry: The cost of a ferry to Orkney varies depending on the season and whether you're bringing a vehicle. A return ticket for a foot passenger typically costs around £15-£25, while taking a car can increase the cost to £60-£100 for a return trip.

- Flight: Flights to Orkney can be relatively affordable, with prices ranging from £40-£100 for a one-way ticket, depending on the time of year and the airline.

- Entry Fees: Many of Orkney's Viking heritage sites have an entry fee, though some sites are free to visit. For example, entry to Skara Brae costs around £9-£12 per adult, while other sites like the Earl's Palace or The Brough of Birsay charge an entry fee of around £5-£7.

- Guided Tours: A guided tour of Orkney's Viking heritage typically costs between £15-£30 per person, depending on the length and depth of the tour.

Exploring the Viking heritage in Orkney is an unforgettable journey that blends history, archaeology, and breathtaking natural landscapes. Whether you're walking among ancient ruins, exploring Viking burial sites, or learning about the influence of the Norse people, Orkney offers a rare opportunity to step back in time and experience the legacy of the Vikings in one of the most captivating corners of Scotland.

Stargazing in Galloway Forest

Galloway Forest, located in the southwest of Scotland, is a hidden gem for stargazers. As one of the UK's most renowned dark sky areas, it offers an unparalleled opportunity to explore the night sky in all its glory. Whether you're an experienced astronomer or someone who simply enjoys stargazing, Galloway Forest is the perfect place to immerse yourself in the wonders of the universe, far from the light pollution of city life.

What to Expect in Galloway Forest for Stargazing

Galloway Forest Park is one of Scotland's largest forests and a designated Dark Sky Park, meaning it is free from excessive artificial lighting and offers some of the best stargazing conditions in the UK. With its remote location and expansive views, the park provides an ideal setting for viewing the Milky Way, spotting constellations, and even catching a glimpse of the Northern Lights during the right conditions.

- Clear, Dark Skies: One of the most important factors for stargazing is the absence of light pollution. Galloway Forest Park offers some of the darkest skies in the UK, allowing stargazers to witness celestial phenomena with minimal interference from artificial lights. On a clear night, you can see thousands of stars, planets, and distant galaxies.

- Meteor Showers: Galloway is a fantastic location for observing meteor showers, particularly during peak times such as the Perseid in August or the Geminid meteor showers in December. The dark skies and the absence of city lights provide the perfect conditions for watching shooting stars streak across the sky.

- The Milky Way: With minimal light pollution, Galloway Forest is a prime location for viewing the Milky Way in all its splendor. The dense band of stars can be clearly seen stretching across the sky, especially on cloudless, moonless nights, making for a truly breathtaking experience.

- Northern Lights: Although rare, the Aurora Borealis or Northern Lights can occasionally be seen from Galloway Forest Park, especially during periods of high solar activity. The dark skies make it an excellent spot for witnessing this natural phenomenon if conditions are right.

What to Explore

Galloway Forest Park offers more than just stargazing. During the day, you can explore the park's expansive landscapes, tranquil lochs, and rugged hills. Here are a few highlights:

- Wildlife Watching: The park is home to a wide range of wildlife, including red deer, otters, and various bird species. There are numerous walking trails and viewpoints that allow you to enjoy both the natural beauty of the forest and the wildlife within it.

- Walking and Hiking Trails: Galloway Forest is crisscrossed with walking and hiking trails, offering a range of paths for all levels of fitness. These trails provide scenic views of the surrounding landscape, and some lead to designated viewpoints perfect for stargazing at night.

- Lochs and Waterfalls: The park is dotted with picturesque lochs and waterfalls, including Loch Trool and Grey Mare's Tail, which are stunning during both the day and night. The tranquil waters and rugged surroundings create a peaceful atmosphere for nature lovers.

- Climbing Merrick Hill: For those who enjoy hiking, climbing Merrick, the highest hill in southern Scotland, offers panoramic views over Galloway Forest and beyond. On a clear day, you can see as far as the Lake District and even Ireland.

What to Expect

When stargazing in Galloway Forest, there are a few things to keep in mind to make the most of your experience:

- Darkness and Silence: The park offers an unparalleled sense of solitude and peace. With little to no artificial light and minimal noise pollution, the dark skies create a perfect environment for stargazing. Expect total silence and stillness under the stars, making for a deeply calming and meditative experience.

- Chilly Nights: Even during the summer months, the nights in Galloway Forest can be cold, especially at higher altitudes. Be sure to bring warm clothing, even if you're visiting during the warmer seasons.

- Remote Location: Galloway Forest is situated in a relatively remote area, so be prepared for a lack of amenities in some parts of the park. There are visitor centers and some facilities, but it's wise to plan ahead for supplies, especially if you're heading to more secluded areas.

- Perfect for Photography: The clear skies and stunning landscapes make Galloway Forest an ideal location for astrophotography. Whether you're capturing the Milky Way or long-exposure shots of star trails, the park offers fantastic opportunities for photographers.

How to Get There

Galloway Forest Park is located in Southwest Scotland, roughly a 1.5-hour drive from Glasgow and Edinburgh. Here's how you can get there:

- By Car: The easiest way to reach Galloway Forest Park is by car. The park is well-connected to major roads, and the drive from either Glasgow or Edinburgh is scenic and straightforward. The A713 road takes you through the heart of the park, and there are several access points to key stargazing locations.

- By Train: If you're coming by train, you can take a train to Dumfries, which is the closest major town to the park. From there, you can hire a car or take a bus to reach the park. The nearest station is in Newton Stewart, a small town near the park.

- By Bus: There are bus services that run to Newton Stewart, and from there, you can take a local taxi to reach the park's designated stargazing spots.

Cost

While the Galloway Forest Park itself is free to visit, there are some costs involved if you're planning to stay or need additional services:

- Entrance Fees: There are no entrance fees for accessing Galloway Forest Park. It is open to the public year-round, and you can explore the park freely.

- Accommodation: Accommodation around Galloway Forest can vary, ranging from camping sites and hostels to holiday cottages and B&Bs. Prices can range from £20-£100 per night, depending on your choice of accommodation and the season.

- Parking Fees: Some parking areas within the park may charge a small fee, typically ranging from £2-£5 for the day, particularly at popular visitor centers.

- Stargazing Equipment: If you don't have your own telescope or binoculars, some local businesses in nearby towns offer stargazing equipment for hire. Prices for a telescope rental can range from £15-£40 per day.

Stargazing in Galloway Forest Park is an awe-inspiring experience, offering the chance to immerse yourself in some of the darkest and clearest skies in the UK. Whether you're an experienced astronomer or just someone who enjoys looking at the stars, Galloway Forest is a magical destination for all. With its serene landscapes, wildlife, and the opportunity to explore Scotland's skies in their purest form, it's a must-visit for anyone seeking to experience the wonders of the night sky.

Whisky Distillery Tours and Tastings in Scotland

Scotland is renowned worldwide for its whisky, and no trip to the country would be complete without exploring its famous whisky distilleries. Whisky, often referred to as "Scotch," is a vital part of Scotland's heritage and culture. A whisky distillery tour not only allows you to experience the craftsmanship behind this iconic drink but also offers the chance to immerse yourself in the history and traditions that make Scottish whisky so unique.

What to Expect at Whisky Distillery Tours

Whisky distillery tours are a fascinating experience for whisky enthusiasts and beginners alike. When you visit a distillery, you can expect a comprehensive look at the whisky-making process, from the mashing of barley to the aging of the spirit in oak casks. Here's what you can expect during a distillery tour:

- Learn About Whisky Production: A guided tour will take you through the whisky-making process, explaining each step in detail. You'll learn how barley is mashed, fermented, distilled, and matured. Distilleries often offer a hands-on experience, allowing you to see the equipment up close, including copper pot stills and oak casks.

- Expert Guides: Knowledgeable guides lead most distillery tours, sharing insights into the history of whisky-making in Scotland, the specific distillery's methods, and the distinct characteristics of different types of whisky.

- Whisky Tastings: At the end of the tour, most distilleries offer tastings where you can sample a range of their whiskies. The tastings give you the opportunity to compare different aged whiskies, cask finishes, and flavor profiles. Many distilleries offer several tiers of tastings, ranging from basic samples to exclusive, premium whiskies.

- Shop for Whisky Souvenirs: Many distilleries have on-site shops where you can purchase exclusive bottles of whisky that are not available in stores. It's a great opportunity to buy unique gifts or take home a special bottle as a reminder of your experience.

- Food Pairings: Some distilleries offer food pairings with whisky tastings, allowing you to experience the unique flavors of whisky alongside Scottish cuisine. From traditional haggis to smoked salmon, the food can enhance the tasting experience.

What to Explore at Whisky Distilleries

A whisky distillery visit offers much more than just the opportunity to taste whisky. Many distilleries are located in picturesque locations, surrounded by scenic landscapes, historic buildings, and tranquil surroundings. Here are a few things you can explore during your visit:

- Historic Distilleries: Some of Scotland's distilleries have centuries of history, dating back to the 18th and 19th centuries. Exploring these distilleries gives you a deep understanding of Scotland's whisky heritage. Notable distilleries, such as Glenfiddich, Macallan, and Glenlivet, offer guided tours where you can learn about their long histories and the families behind their success.

- Cask Rooms and Warehouses: Many distilleries have extensive cask rooms where the whisky matures. The smell of the aging whisky in these warehouses is distinctive and can be an immersive part of the tour. Some distilleries allow you to see the casks up close and learn about the aging process and how it influences the flavor of the whisky.

- Whisky Making Workshops: Certain distilleries offer workshops where you can try your hand at whisky blending or cask tasting. These workshops offer a more in-depth, hands-on experience for those who want to get involved in the whisky-making process.

- Whisky Museums: Some distilleries have dedicated museums where you can explore the rich history of whisky-making, featuring old distilling equipment, historical photos, and exhibits about the evolution of the industry.

What to Expect on a Whisky Distillery Tour

- Atmosphere: Expect a welcoming, often cozy atmosphere. Distilleries are typically located in beautiful, serene locations, ranging from remote highland valleys to coastal regions. The buildings themselves are often centuries old, contributing to the charm of the experience.

- Taste Different Varieties: Distillery tours generally allow you to taste a variety of whiskies, ranging from younger, lighter expressions to older, more complex bottles. Some distilleries may also offer limited-edition releases that you can sample.

- Storytelling: Distillery tours often involve a mix of storytelling and educational content. Guides will explain the history of whisky, how the distillery was founded, and its significance to the local community and the whisky industry as a whole.

- A Unique Experience: Every distillery tour offers a unique experience based on the distillery's location, style, and approach to whisky production. Some may feature innovative production techniques, while others stick to traditional methods passed down through generations.

- Tasting Etiquette: Many distilleries encourage a slow and deliberate approach to whisky tasting, where you'll savor each sip, considering the aromas, taste, and finish. It's a relaxing and educational experience that allows you to appreciate the nuances of each whisky.

How to Get to Whisky Distilleries

Scotland's whisky distilleries are spread across the country, with the most famous regions being Speyside, Islay, and the Highlands. Here's how to get to some of Scotland's iconic whisky regions:

- By Car: The best way to visit whisky distilleries is by car, especially if you're traveling to multiple distilleries in a region. Most distilleries are easily accessible via major roads, but some may require a bit of a drive through picturesque country lanes. Many distilleries have parking facilities for visitors.

- By Train: Some distilleries are accessible by train, especially those located near larger towns. For example, Speyside has direct train connections from Aberdeen or Inverness, with several distilleries located close to the railway stations.

- Guided Whisky Tours: Many tour operators in Scotland offer guided whisky tours, which include transportation to several distilleries in one region. This is a great option for those who want to enjoy the experience without worrying about driving.

- By Plane: If you're traveling from further afield, there are airports in Aberdeen, Edinburgh, and Glasgow that serve as gateways to whisky regions. From these cities, you can easily reach the whisky distilleries by train or car.

Cost of Whisky Distillery Tours

The cost of a whisky distillery tour can vary depending on the distillery, the type of tour, and whether you're doing a basic tour or a premium experience. Here are some general pricing guidelines:

- Standard Tours: A basic distillery tour typically costs between £10-£20 per person, which includes a guided tour and a tasting of a few whiskies. Some distilleries offer more affordable options for self-guided tours.

- Premium or Exclusive Tours: Premium or private tours, which may include a more in-depth look at the distilling process, tastings of rare whiskies, and sometimes a meal, can cost anywhere from £30-£100 or more per person.

- Masterclasses and Workshops: Special whisky masterclasses or blending workshops can be more expensive, ranging from £40-£150 per person, depending on the distillery.

- Tasting Fees: Some distilleries charge separately for tastings, with prices typically starting at around £5-£10 per person. Premium tastings may be more expensive.

- Whisky Bottles: Don't forget the cost of buying whisky. Bottles at distilleries can range from £30-£300 depending on the rarity and age of the whisky.

A whisky distillery tour in Scotland is a must-do for anyone who loves whisky or simply wants to explore the country's rich history and culture. Whether you're visiting a historic distillery in Speyside, tasting peat-heavy whiskies on Islay, or experiencing the highland craft in the Highlands, each distillery offers its own unique insight into Scotland's most famous drink. With beautiful landscapes, expert guides, and an opportunity to sample some of the finest whiskies in the world, a whisky distillery tour is an unforgettable experience for any visitor to Scotland.

Chapter 7: Scottish Cuisine and Dining

Traditional Scottish Dishes: Haggis, Cullen Skink, and Shortbread

Scotland's culinary tradition is deeply rooted in its history and culture, offering dishes that are hearty, flavorful, and often unique to the region. Here's a closer look at three classic Scottish dishes: Haggis, Cullen Skink, and Shortbread. These dishes embody the essence of Scottish cooking, using local ingredients and time-honored methods.

Haggis

Ingredients

Haggis is a traditional Scottish dish made from sheep's offal (heart, liver, and lungs), combined with oats, suet, onions, and spices. It's traditionally encased in a sheep's stomach (though synthetic casings are often used today). The dish is seasoned with salt, pepper, and a variety of spices such as nutmeg, coriander, and cayenne pepper, giving it a rich, savory flavor.

- Sheep's offal (heart, liver, and lungs)
- Oats
- Suet (animal fat)
- Onion
- Spices (salt, pepper, nutmeg, coriander, cayenne pepper)
- Broth (usually stock or water)

Where to Get It

Haggis can be found in most traditional Scottish restaurants and pubs across Scotland. It's especially popular during Burns Night (January 25), a celebration of the poet Robert Burns, who famously wrote a poem about haggis.

- Edinburgh: The Royal Mile is lined with pubs and restaurants serving haggis, with The Royal McGregor offering a particularly popular version.
- Glasgow: The Shandon Belles restaurant is known for its classic haggis served with neeps and tatties (mashed turnips and potatoes).
- Isle of Skye: Visit the Skye Food Co. for a more contemporary take on this traditional dish.

Cost

- Haggis Plate: £8–£15 per serving, depending on the establishment and whether it's served as part of a full meal.

- Haggis Takeaway: You can also buy pre-cooked haggis from supermarkets like Tesco or Marks & Spencer, with prices typically ranging from £5 to £10.

Cullen Skink

Ingredients

Cullen Skink is a rich and creamy soup originating from the town of Cullen in the northeast of Scotland. Traditionally made with smoked haddock, potatoes, onions, and milk or cream, this comforting dish is perfect for chilly Scottish days.

- Smoked haddock
- Potatoes
- Onion
- Milk or cream
- Butter
- Parsley (for garnish)

Where to Get It

Cullen Skink is a dish that you'll find in many Scottish coastal towns, particularly those close to where the fish is caught. It's commonly served in restaurants along the Moray Firth, where the dish originated.

- Cullen: The Cullen Bay Hotel is the birthplace of this iconic dish and is the best place to sample an authentic Cullen Skink.
- Edinburgh: The Mussel & Steak Bar in the city center serves a delicious take on Cullen Skink.
- Inverness: You can also find great versions of this soup in local seafood restaurants, such as The Kitchen.

Cost

- Cullen Skink Soup: £6–£12 per bowl, depending on the restaurant and whether it's served as a starter or a main.
- Cullen Skink at Supermarkets: Ready-made versions can be purchased at many supermarkets, typically costing between £3 and £5 per serving.

Shortbread

Ingredients

Shortbread is a beloved Scottish biscuit (cookie) made from butter, sugar, and flour. The texture is crisp yet melt-in-your-mouth tender, and it's often served during tea time or as a snack. Some variations might include rice flour for added crispness.

- Butter

- Sugar (white or caster sugar)

- Plain flour

- Rice flour (optional, for texture)

Where to Get It

Shortbread is ubiquitous across Scotland, and you can find it in nearly every bakery, supermarket, and café. It's a popular souvenir for visitors, and many high-end brands offer beautifully packaged versions for gifting.

- Edinburgh: The Edinburgh Larder offers freshly made shortbread with a traditional flavor.

- Perth: The Scottish Shortbread Company produces artisan shortbread that can be found in local shops and online.

- Glasgow: The Tunnock's brand, famous for its caramel wafers, also offers traditional shortbread biscuits.

Cost

- Shortbread: £2–£8 per packet, depending on the brand and packaging. For example, premium shortbread brands like Walkers or Dean's typically range from £4 to £8 for a box, while supermarket versions like Tesco or Sainsbury's offer more affordable options around £2 to £3.

Scotland's traditional dishes offer a deep dive into the country's history, flavors, and culinary techniques. Haggis represents the heart of Scottish cuisine, Cullen Skink highlights the country's coastal influences, and Shortbread is a sweet treat that accompanies Scots in their daily lives. Whether you're trying these dishes at a local restaurant, buying them at a supermarket, or making them at home, these iconic foods are a perfect way to experience the true taste of Scotland.

Best pubs and restaurants across Scotland

The Royal McGregor (Edinburgh)

- What to Expect:

The Royal McGregor is a traditional Scottish pub offering a warm and welcoming atmosphere. Known for its hearty meals and extensive whisky selection, it serves classic Scottish fare like haggis, neeps, and tatties, along with comfort food options such as steak pies and fish and chips. The pub often features live music, making it a great spot to enjoy a pint while soaking in some local culture.

- How to Get There:

Located on the Royal Mile, it's easily accessible from the Edinburgh Castle and the city center. If you're traveling by public transport, you can take a bus or tram to the nearest stop at the Royal Mile and walk for a few minutes to reach the pub.

- Cost:

Expect to pay around £12–£20 for a main dish, with some traditional meals like haggis costing less. Drinks range from £4–£7 for a pint of local ale.

Shandon Belles (Glasgow)

- What to Expect:

Shandon Belles is a beloved spot for those craving traditional Scottish dishes, particularly seafood. The warm and casual pub atmosphere makes it perfect for a relaxed meal. You'll find classics like Cullen Skink (a creamy smoked haddock soup) and a variety of fresh, locally sourced seafood dishes. It's known for friendly service and excellent value.

- How to Get There:

Situated in the heart of Glasgow's West End, Shandon Belles is easily reachable by subway. The nearest subway station is Kelvinhall, which is a 5-minute walk from the pub. Alternatively, local buses also pass through the area.

- Cost:

Main dishes range from £10–£20. The seafood options can be a bit more expensive, depending on the catch of the day, with a bowl of Cullen Skink priced around £6.

The Three Chimneys (Isle of Skye)

- What to Expect:

The Three Chimneys is a Michelin-recognized restaurant offering a fine dining experience with a focus on local, seasonal ingredients. Located in a picturesque setting with breathtaking views of the Isle of Skye, it is perfect for those looking to enjoy the best of Scottish cuisine. The menu features innovative dishes made from fresh fish, shellfish, game, and local produce. Expect exceptional service and an intimate atmosphere.

- How to Get There:

Located on the northern part of the Isle of Skye, near Dunvegan, The Three Chimneys is a 10-minute drive from the village. There are also local buses that pass through the area, but renting a car is the most convenient way to get there.

- Cost:

Expect to pay around £30–£60 per person for a main course, with tasting menus and multi-course options costing upwards of £90 per person.

The Silver Darling (Aberdeen)

- What to Expect:

Located on the edge of Aberdeen's bustling harbor, The Silver Darling specializes in fresh seafood, offering stunning views of the North Sea. Its menu showcases a variety of local fish and shellfish, with dishes like crab cakes, lobster, and smoked salmon being the highlights. The restaurant has a sophisticated yet relaxed atmosphere, making it an ideal choice for a special occasion or a romantic dinner.

- How to Get There:

The Silver Darling is located in the Aberdeen Harbor area, around a 15-minute walk from the city center. Public transport is available, with bus services to nearby stops, and taxis are also easily accessible.

- Cost:

Expect to pay around £15–£30 for a main dish. Seafood platters and lobster dishes can be more expensive, with prices ranging from £25–£50, depending on what's on the menu.

Whisky Tastings and Food Pairings in Scotland

Scotland is renowned for its whisky, often referred to as "the water of life" or "uisge beatha" in Gaelic. Whisky tastings paired with food offer a wonderful way to immerse yourself in Scotland's rich cultural heritage while savoring some of its finest flavors. Here's an overview of what to expect and how to enjoy whisky tastings and food pairings.

What to Expect

Whisky tastings in Scotland are immersive experiences where you'll have the opportunity to sample a range of Scotch whiskies, typically divided into categories such as single malts, blended whiskies, and cask-strength options. Tastings are usually conducted by knowledgeable guides or distillery experts, who will explain the distillation process, the importance of terroir, and the unique characteristics of different whiskies. Many tastings also allow you to explore the history behind some of Scotland's oldest and most famous distilleries.

During these events, the whisky is often paired with foods to enhance the tasting experience. Pairings can range from light appetizers to multi-course meals, designed to complement and bring out the subtle flavors of the whisky.

Food Pairings with Whisky

Different types of whisky lend themselves to specific food pairings. The key to a great whisky and food pairing is finding complementary flavors that enhance the tasting experience.

Single Malt Scotch

- Best Paired With:
  - Cheeses: Strong cheeses like blue cheese or smoked cheeses.
  - Charcuterie: Rich cured meats such as salami or prosciutto.
  - Dark Chocolate: The rich bitterness of dark chocolate contrasts beautifully with the smoky or peaty flavors of some single malts.
- Recommended Whisky: A smoky Islay malt like Laphroaig or Lagavulin.

Blended Scotch

- Best Paired With:
  - Smoked Salmon: The delicate smokiness of salmon works well with the smooth and balanced notes of blended Scotch.
  - Nuts: Almonds, walnuts, and hazelnuts complement the smoother flavor profiles of blended whiskies.
  - Apple Tarts: The light fruitiness of apple tarts can balance the sweetness in blended whiskies.
- Recommended Whisky: Famous blends like Johnnie Walker or Chivas Regal.

Cask Strength Whisky

- Best Paired With:
  - Steak or Grilled Meats: The bold, intense flavor of cask-strength whisky matches perfectly with rich, grilled meats.
  - Rich Desserts: Pairing with dark fruits like cherries or spiced cakes can create a memorable balance.
  - Blue Cheese: The strong and pungent flavor of blue cheese pairs beautifully with the intensity of cask-strength whisky.
- Recommended Whisky: Cask strength options from distilleries like Aberlour, Glenfiddich, or Macallan.

Where to Experience Whisky Tastings and Food Pairings

Scotland boasts numerous distilleries, bars, and restaurants that offer whisky tastings paired with food. Some top locations to consider are:

The Scotch Whisky Experience (Edinburgh)

Located on the Royal Mile, this interactive visitor center offers a range of whisky tasting experiences, including food pairings with local delicacies. It's an excellent introduction to Scotch whisky, perfect for beginners and connoisseurs alike.

Macallan Distillery (Speyside)

Known for its rich, sherried single malts, the Macallan distillery offers curated whisky tastings with gourmet food pairings. Guests can enjoy a tasting session in their modern visitor center, followed by a delicious lunch or dinner.

Ardbeg Distillery (Islay)

For fans of peaty whisky, Ardbeg on Islay offers one of the most iconic tasting experiences. Their whiskies are paired with foods like smoked salmon and shellfish to complement the bold smoky flavors.

The Balmoral Hotel (Edinburgh)

If you want to enjoy a luxurious whisky experience, the Balmoral Hotel offers whisky tastings paired with fine dining in its Michelin-starred restaurant, Number One.

Aberlour Distillery (Speyside)

Aberlour's food pairing experiences are often held at their distillery in Speyside, known for its rich, sherried single malts. Guests can pair their tastings with Scottish cheeses, smoked meats, and dark chocolate.

How to Participate

Many distilleries offer pre-booked whisky tasting tours with food pairings, which can be booked online or by contacting the venue directly. Some tours include a guided walk through the distillery, an overview of the whisky-making process, and tastings of their finest expressions. The food pairing experiences may include a set menu with wine or whisky pairings, and many venues also offer private whisky tasting sessions tailored to specific preferences.

Cost

The cost of whisky tastings with food pairings varies depending on the venue, the type of whisky, and the complexity of the food pairing.

- Basic Tastings: Expect to pay £10–£30 for a standard whisky tasting, which may include 3–4 different whiskies.

- Premium Experiences: For exclusive cask-strength whiskies or multi-course meals paired with whisky, the cost can range from £50–£100 per person.

- Private Tasting Experiences: These can cost upwards of £150 per person, especially at high-end distilleries or Michelin-starred restaurants.

Whisky tastings with food pairings offer a rich and flavorful journey through Scotland's culinary and drink traditions. Whether you're savoring a smoky Islay malt with a plate of charcuterie, or enjoying a Speyside whisky alongside fresh seafood, pairing food with whisky enhances the experience and allows you to appreciate the complexities of Scotland's world-famous spirit.

Exploring Local Markets and Food Festivals in Scotland

Scotland is a treasure trove of unique flavors and local produce, and one of the best ways to experience this is by visiting the country's vibrant markets and food festivals. These markets and festivals not only offer an abundance of fresh, local ingredients but also provide a chance to immerse yourself in Scotland's rich culinary heritage and meet passionate food producers. Here's a guide to exploring Scotland's markets and food festivals.

What to Expect

When visiting local markets in Scotland, you'll be treated to a wide array of fresh, locally sourced produce. From artisanal cheeses, smoked fish, and fresh meats to hand-crafted chocolates, jams, and baked goods, the variety is immense. You'll find many of Scotland's famed products, such as locally caught seafood, venison, Aberdeen Angus beef, and the iconic haggis. Additionally, many of the markets feature local arts and crafts, giving visitors a complete Scottish experience.

At food festivals, you can expect to sample dishes from renowned chefs, discover street food from around the world, and take part in cooking demonstrations, tastings, and competitions. Food festivals in Scotland are often set against stunning backdrops, from the Scottish Highlands to coastal villages, making for a delightful combination of food, culture, and landscape.

Popular Local Markets in Scotland

Edinburgh Farmers' Market

 Located beneath Edinburgh Castle, this is one of Scotland's most famous farmers' markets. Open every Saturday, it offers an excellent selection of organic and locally sourced produce. Expect to find everything from fresh Scottish strawberries and artisan breads to locally made cheeses and craft beers.

Glasgow's Barras Market

 This iconic market has been operating since the 1920s and offers a mix of fresh produce, clothing, antiques, and local specialties. A visit to the Barras is a trip into Glasgow's cultural heritage, and it's a great place to try local delicacies like haggis, tattie scones, and Scotch pies.

St. Andrews Farmers' Market

 Held on the first Saturday of each month, this market showcases the best of Fife's local produce. You can sample fresh seafood, artisan cheeses, and hand-made chutneys, as well as baked goods from local bakers.

Aberdeen's Artisans' Market

Taking place on various weekends throughout the year, this market celebrates the North East of Scotland's best food producers and craftspeople. From fishmongers selling fresh catches of the day to independent chocolatiers, it's a great place to explore the flavors of the region.

Perth Farmers' Market

Known for its scenic location along the River Tay, Perth's farmers' market is held every Saturday. Expect to find locally grown vegetables, meats, and cheeses as well as specialties like smoked salmon and haggis.

Notable Food Festivals in Scotland

Edinburgh Food Festival

This annual festival, typically held in July, celebrates the best of Scottish food and drink. With a combination of chef demonstrations, tastings, food trucks, and live entertainment, the festival is a must-visit for food lovers. It's the perfect place to sample traditional Scottish dishes like haggis and Cullen skink, as well as discover innovative new food trends.

Scottish Seafood Festival

Held in the picturesque town of Anstruther in Fife, this festival celebrates Scotland's world-famous seafood. Expect to enjoy fresh oysters, smoked salmon, and other locally caught fish. The festival also hosts cooking demonstrations and boat tours, giving you a chance to learn more about Scotland's fishing industry.

The Royal Highland Show

Held annually in Edinburgh, this is one of Scotland's largest agricultural events, attracting thousands of visitors. While it's focused on the country's agricultural industries, food lovers can enjoy a range of Scottish food stalls offering traditional and contemporary dishes, local meats, and craft beverages.

The Fife Food Festival

A celebration of Fife's diverse culinary offerings, the Fife Food Festival, typically held in October, features local farmers, bakers, and chefs. It's an excellent opportunity to sample local cheeses, fresh fruit and vegetables, and meats, as well as take part in cooking workshops and tastings.

The Mull Food Festival

The Isle of Mull hosts an annual food festival that highlights the island's natural produce, from seafood and venison to dairy products and jams. Visitors can take part in guided tours to local food producers, cooking workshops, and taste the island's delights at the various food stalls.

Glasgow's Food and Drink Festival

A celebration of Glasgow's growing food scene, this festival brings together some of the city's top chefs, local food producers, and street food vendors. Expect to find an impressive variety of dishes, from Scottish staples to international cuisine, served up in a lively, vibrant atmosphere.

What to Explore

Aside from sampling food at markets and festivals, many food events offer additional opportunities to explore the surrounding areas. Farmers' markets are often held in scenic outdoor locations, so you can enjoy the beautiful landscapes of Edinburgh, the Highlands, or the coastal regions while you shop. Additionally, many food festivals are hosted in areas of cultural significance, such as historic castles, seaside towns, or bustling city squares, allowing you to explore the heritage of Scotland while indulging in its culinary offerings.

For those interested in learning more about Scotland's food production, many markets and festivals also offer guided tours or workshops. You can tour local farms, visit distilleries for whisky tastings, or attend cooking classes to learn how to prepare traditional Scottish dishes.

How to Get There

Most Scottish towns and cities are well-connected by public transportation, making it easy to get to markets and festivals. If you're traveling to a larger city like Edinburgh or Glasgow, both cities have efficient bus, train, and tram networks. For more remote markets and festivals, like those in the Highlands or on the islands, it's recommended to drive or take a local tour to reach the event.

Cost

Costs for local markets are generally quite affordable, with many markets offering a variety of options at different price points. Farmers' markets often have free entry, and you can spend as much or as little as you like depending on what you're buying. Food festivals, on the other hand, can range from free entry to ticketed events, with prices typically ranging from £5 to £20 for general entry or for access to specific activities, tastings, or workshops. For a more immersive experience, food tours or special food and drink pairings may cost anywhere from £30 to £100 per person, depending on the event.

Exploring Scotland's local markets and food festivals is a fantastic way to experience the country's rich culinary heritage. Whether you're wandering through an open-air farmers' market, sampling artisanal cheeses, or attending a lively food festival, you'll discover the flavors that make Scottish cuisine so unique. With its stunning scenery, vibrant food scene, and welcoming local producers, Scotland's food markets and festivals offer something for every food lover.

Chapter 8: Accommodation in Scotland

Luxury hotels and historic castles

The Balmoral Hotel, Edinburgh

What to Expect

The Balmoral Hotel is one of Edinburgh's most iconic landmarks, offering a combination of luxury, elegance, and traditional Scottish hospitality. Situated in the heart of Edinburgh, with stunning views of Edinburgh Castle and the Old Town, this five-star hotel boasts lavish rooms, a Michelin-starred restaurant, a luxurious spa, and a heated indoor pool. Expect world-class service and refined interiors blending Scottish heritage with modern luxury. The hotel's signature features include the famous clock tower, a symbol of Edinburgh, and the stylish Palm Court for afternoon tea.

How to Get There

The Balmoral is conveniently located just a short walk from Edinburgh Waverley Railway Station, making it easily accessible by train. It is also well-served by buses, trams, and taxis. For those flying into Edinburgh, the hotel is about a 25-minute drive from Edinburgh Airport.

Cost

Room rates at The Balmoral start from around £350 per night for a standard room. Rates for suites and deluxe rooms can exceed £1,000 per night, depending on the season and room type. Dining at the Michelin-starred restaurant and spa treatments are additional costs.

Gleneagles Hotel, Auchterarder

What to Expect

Gleneagles is a luxurious resort nestled in the heart of the Scottish Highlands. Famous for its championship golf courses, including the Ryder Cup venue, Gleneagles also offers a world-class spa, fine dining, equestrian activities, and a range of outdoor pursuits like clay pigeon shooting, falconry, and off-roading. Expect elegant rooms and suites, top-tier service, and a setting that blends traditional Scottish architecture with modern comfort. The hotel is an ideal escape for those seeking relaxation, adventure, and indulgence in the countryside.

How to Get There

Gleneagles Hotel is located in Auchterarder, around 40 minutes' drive from both Edinburgh and Glasgow. The hotel is easily accessible by car and is also reachable via train from Edinburgh or Glasgow to Gleneagles Railway Station, which is just a short ride from the hotel.

Cost

Prices at Gleneagles start from around £350 per night for a standard room, with suites and larger rooms starting at £500 per night or more. The resort offers various packages that can include activities and meals, with prices ranging from £500 to £1,500 per night depending on the level of luxury and the experiences included.

The Old Course Hotel, St Andrews

What to Expect

Located on the world-renowned Old Course golf course in St Andrews, this five-star hotel is a dream destination for golf enthusiasts and those seeking luxury by the sea. The Old Course Hotel offers elegantly appointed rooms with stunning views of the golf course or the Firth of Forth. Guests can expect a Michelin-starred restaurant, the famous Road Hole Bar, and a luxurious spa with a range of treatments. Additionally, the hotel offers bespoke golf packages, making it the ultimate place to stay for golfers.

How to Get There

The Old Course Hotel is in St Andrews, approximately an hour and a half's drive from Edinburgh and about two hours from Glasgow. St Andrews is well-connected by road, and the nearest train station is Leuchars, about 7 miles away. A taxi or bus service is available from Leuchars to the hotel.

Cost

Room rates at The Old Course Hotel start around £400 per night for a standard room. Deluxe rooms, suites, and packages including golf tee times can cost upwards of £600 to £1,500 per night. Special golf packages that include accommodation, rounds of golf, and spa treatments are available for more exclusive experiences.

Camping and glamping options

Loch Lomond Campsites

What to Expect

Loch Lomond Campsites offer a range of scenic spots perfect for traditional camping and caravanning. Located near the stunning Loch Lomond and within Loch Lomond & The Trossachs National Park, the campsite provides a picturesque backdrop with plenty of opportunities for hiking, fishing, and water sports. Expect well-maintained facilities such as hot showers, picnic areas, and accessible paths. Many sites also offer direct access to the loch, ideal for boaters and nature lovers.

What to Explore

- Explore the surrounding Loch Lomond & The Trossachs National Park, renowned for its natural beauty and wildlife.

- Water activities like kayaking, canoeing, and fishing on Loch Lomond.

- Scenic hikes along the West Highland Way or nearby forest trails.

- Nearby attractions like Balloch Castle and the village of Luss.

How to Get There

The Loch Lomond Campsites are accessible by car from Glasgow, around a 30-minute drive. The site is also well-served by public transport, with nearby bus services and train stations in Balloch.

Cost

Tent pitches typically start from £15-£25 per night, depending on location and season. Prices for glamping pods and cabins are higher, starting around £50 per night. Rates for motorhomes and caravans vary between £20-£40 per night.

Glenmore Campsite, Cairngorms National Park

What to Expect

Nestled in the heart of Cairngorms National Park, Glenmore Campsite is a beautiful location that offers a range of camping options, from traditional tent pitches to motorhome spaces and luxury glamping pods. Set against the stunning backdrop of the Cairngorm mountains and close to Loch Morlich, expect an outdoor experience with access to great hiking, cycling, and water activities. The campsite offers excellent facilities, including a shop, laundry, and modern shower blocks.

What to Explore

- Loch Morlich for swimming, sailing, and paddleboarding.

- Hike the Cairngorms, including the popular route to Cairn Gorm summit.

- Explore the nearby Glenmore Forest and enjoy forest walks.

- Visit the Cairngorm Reindeer Centre to see the famous wild reindeer.

How to Get There

The campsite is located near Aviemore in the Cairngorms National Park. It's about 40 minutes by car from Inverness and 1.5 hours from Aberdeen. Public transport options include a bus from Aviemore, though driving is the most convenient way to reach the site.

Cost

Tent pitches generally start from £15-£20 per night, with glamping pods priced from £60-£80 per night depending on the season and accommodation type. Prices for motorhome pitches start around £25 per night.

The Canopy & Stars Glamping, Fife

What to Expect

The Canopy & Stars Glamping site in Fife offers a luxurious outdoor experience with unique and stylish glamping accommodations. The site features treehouses, yurts, and bell tents equipped with comfortable furnishings, wood-burning stoves, and en-suite bathrooms. Expect a peaceful retreat in nature, with an emphasis on sustainability and eco-friendly practices. The glamping site is perfect for those seeking a relaxing getaway with a touch of luxury and tranquility, along with stunning views of the Scottish countryside.

What to Explore

- Explore the nearby Fife coastal path, known for its picturesque views.

- Visit St Andrews, home to historic architecture and the world-famous golf course.

- Discover the medieval Dunfermline Abbey and Palace.

- Explore the village of Falkland, where the Falkland Palace and Gardens are located.

How to Get There

The site is located in the Fife region of Scotland, about an hour's drive from Edinburgh and around 90 minutes from Glasgow. The site can be reached by car or public transport, with train services to Leven and bus options from there.

Cost

The cost of glamping accommodation at The Canopy & Stars starts from around £120-£200 per night, depending on the type of glamping experience and season. Rates for more luxurious units or peak times may be higher.

Chapter 9: Getting Around Scotland

Public Transportation in Scotland: Trains, Buses, and Ferries

Scotland offers a comprehensive public transportation system that makes traveling across the country convenient, affordable, and scenic. Whether you're exploring bustling cities, the rugged Highlands, or the islands, Scotland's trains, buses, and ferries are well-connected and efficient.

Trains

Scotland boasts an extensive and reliable rail network, connecting major cities, towns, and tourist destinations across the country. The national train system is operated by ScotRail, and services extend from urban centers to remote areas. Trains are comfortable, and many routes offer beautiful views of the countryside, especially when traveling to the Highlands or along the West Coast.

Key Routes and Destinations:

- Edinburgh to Glasgow: The two largest cities in Scotland are just 45 minutes apart by train, making for a quick and easy commute.

- Edinburgh to Inverness: Journey through the scenic Scottish Highlands, with travel times of around 3.5 hours.

- Glasgow to Fort William: Explore the West Highland Line, one of the most scenic train routes in the world, heading to Fort William.

- Edinburgh to Aberdeen: A direct route that connects Scotland's capital with the city of granite, Aberdeen.

- The Jacobite Steam Train: A famous tourist route from Fort William to Mallaig, featured in the Harry Potter films as the Hogwarts Express.

What to Expect:

- Comfortable seating with Wi-Fi available on most trains.

- Services range from frequent commuter trains to long-distance scenic routes.

- Trains are punctual, and timetables are available via the ScotRail website or app.

How to Get There: Train stations are located in all major cities and towns, with well-signposted platforms and ticket offices. Tickets can be purchased at stations, online, or via mobile apps.

Cost: Train fares vary depending on the route, time of booking, and class. A journey between major cities such as Edinburgh and Glasgow may cost around £5-£15 one-way. Long-distance trains like Edinburgh to Inverness can cost from £20-£50, but booking in advance can secure cheaper rates.

Buses

Buses are an excellent way to get around Scotland, especially for smaller towns, remote areas, and locations that are less accessible by train. The bus network is extensive, with Stagecoach and Citylink being the main operators for intercity and regional routes. Local bus services in cities and towns are also frequent and reliable.

Key Routes and Destinations:

- Glasgow to Edinburgh: Frequent intercity buses run every 30 minutes between these cities, with affordable fares starting from as low as £5 one-way.

- Stirling to Oban: Travel across central Scotland, heading toward the west coast, with a scenic bus ride that takes around 2.5 hours.

- Inverness to Ullapool: Head into the Highlands for views of lochs and mountains with Citylink buses.

What to Expect:

- Comfortable coaches with Wi-Fi, charging points, and large windows for scenic views.

- Buses are an affordable way to reach remote destinations, such as the Isle of Skye or other islands.

- Expect to see local bus services within cities and towns, offering frequent routes and stops.

How to Get There: Buses depart from major bus stations in cities, such as Buchanan Bus Station in Glasgow and St. Andrew Square Bus Station in Edinburgh. Tickets can be purchased online, at ticket machines, or directly from the driver.

Cost: Bus fares range from £2-£10 for short journeys within cities and towns. Longer-distance routes can cost £10-£30, depending on the distance and the route. Discounts may be available for advanced bookings or multi-ride tickets.

Ferries

Scotland is home to some of the most stunning islands in Europe, and ferries are a popular way to reach them. The ferry network is managed by several providers, with Caledonian MacBrayne (CalMac) being the primary operator for routes to the Hebrides, Isle of Skye, and other islands.

Key Routes and Destinations:

- Mallaig to Skye: A short ferry crossing that takes you to the Isle of Skye, a must-visit destination in the Highlands.

- Oban to Mull: A scenic ferry route that connects the mainland with the Isle of Mull, offering stunning coastal views.

- Glenelg to Skye: A smaller, more historic ferry crossing to Skye.

- Uig to Tarbert (Harris): Ferries that connect the Isle of Skye to the Outer Hebrides.

What to Expect:

- Ferries vary from large vessels with amenities such as cafes and seating areas to smaller, more intimate ferries for shorter routes.

- Expect scenic journeys, with plenty of opportunities to spot wildlife like seals, dolphins, and seabirds.

- Some ferries allow for vehicle transport, while others are for foot passengers only.

How to Get There: Ferries depart from ports such as Oban, Mallaig, and Uig. Reservations are often recommended, especially during peak tourist seasons.

Cost: Ferry fares depend on the route, vessel, and whether you're taking a vehicle. Passenger-only fares start at around £5-£10 one-way, while fares for cars can range from £20-£50, depending on the route.

Whether you're hopping on a train to explore the Highlands, catching a bus to remote villages, or taking a ferry to one of Scotland's stunning islands, public transportation offers a reliable and scenic way to explore this beautiful country. Affordable, comfortable, and well-connected, Scotland's transportation network ensures you can easily reach your next adventure.

Renting a Car for the Highland Routes and Isle of Skye

Renting a car in Scotland is one of the best ways to explore the vast beauty of the Highlands and the Isle of Skye. With its winding roads, stunning landscapes, and remote areas, having your own vehicle allows you to fully immerse yourself in Scotland's natural wonders. Whether you're planning to navigate the rugged terrains of the Highlands or discover the enchanting beauty of Skye, driving gives you the flexibility to stop at scenic viewpoints, hidden gems, and charming villages along the way.

What to Expect

When renting a car in Scotland, especially for trips to the Highlands and Isle of Skye, you can expect:

- Scenic Drives: The Scottish Highlands and Isle of Skye boast some of the most scenic drives in the world. You'll drive along narrow roads with breathtaking views of mountains, lochs, and coastlines. Be prepared for winding single-track roads, especially in more remote areas, where you may encounter sheep or wildlife crossing the roads.

- Remote Areas: Many of Scotland's most beautiful locations are remote and not easily accessible by public transportation. Renting a car allows you to explore places like Glen Etive, the Fairy Pools on Skye, and the vast wilderness of the Cairngorms National Park at your own pace.

- Weather Variability: The weather in the Highlands can be unpredictable. Prepare for rain, fog, or sunshine depending on the season. Your rental car will likely be equipped with air conditioning and heating, but it's always best to bring warm and waterproof clothing, especially if you're driving in winter.

- Narrow Roads and Single-Track Lanes: Many roads in the Highlands, especially those leading to remote areas like Skye, are narrow and single-lane, with passing places for cars to take turns. Be cautious and patient, and always drive at a safe speed.

- Driving on the Left: Scotland follows the left-hand driving system. If you're not accustomed to this, take time to familiarize yourself with local driving rules and road signs before heading out.

What to Explore

By renting a car, you have the freedom to explore some of Scotland's most iconic and lesser-known spots:

- The North Coast 500: This scenic route is one of the most famous driving tours in the UK, taking you through the northern Highlands. You'll pass stunning coastal landscapes, castles, whisky distilleries, and quaint villages.

- Isle of Skye: Known for its dramatic landscapes, Skye is a must-see destination. With a car, you can easily explore the island's iconic sites, including the Old Man of Storr, the Fairy Pools, the Quiraing, and the scenic town of Portree.

- Glen Etive: Famous for its stunning views and location in several films, including Skyfall, Glen Etive is best explored by car. The drive is an adventure in itself, with awe-inspiring views of the rugged mountain ranges.

- Loch Ness: Driving around Loch Ness gives you a chance to explore the famed loch, visit Urquhart Castle, and search for the elusive Nessie. The road around the loch offers beautiful views, especially on clear days.

- Cairngorms National Park: A large national park that offers a mix of wildlife, outdoor activities, and picturesque scenery. You can drive to some of its highlights, including Aviemore and the Cairngorm Mountains.

How to Get There

Renting a car is easy in Scotland, with major cities like Edinburgh and Glasgow offering multiple rental services at the airports and city centers. Inverness, the gateway to the Highlands, also has plenty of car rental options.

- Edinburgh or Glasgow Airports: Both airports have major car rental providers, including Avis, Enterprise, Hertz, and Europcar. From these locations, you can easily access the main highways leading to the Highlands and the Isle of Skye.

- Inverness Airport: Located closer to the Highlands, this airport is another convenient starting point if you're heading straight to the northern regions of Scotland. Rental services are available directly at the airport.

- Driving to Skye: To reach the Isle of Skye by car, head to Kyle of Lochalsh from the mainland, where the Skye Bridge connects you to the island. From there, you can drive along Skye's roads to reach popular destinations like Portree and the Fairy Pools.

Cost

The cost of renting a car in Scotland depends on the size of the vehicle, the duration of the rental, and the season. Here's a general breakdown:

- Economy or Compact Car: From £20-£50 per day.

- Mid-Range or SUV: From £50-£100 per day. An SUV is highly recommended for navigating more rugged terrain, especially in remote Highland areas.

- Luxury or Larger Vehicles: From £100 per day and above.

Insurance and Extras:

- Expect to pay an additional fee for insurance, GPS, or child seats, which can range from £10-£25 per day.

- Fuel costs will depend on your route, with the price of petrol averaging around £1.30-£1.50 per liter.

Additional Tips:

- Book in Advance: To get the best deals, especially during peak tourist season, book your car rental ahead of time.

- Driver's Age: Most rental companies require drivers to be at least 21 years old, with a valid driver's license. Drivers under 25 may face an additional young driver surcharge.

- Fuel Policy: Ensure you know the fuel policy for your rental. Most companies operate on a full-to-full policy, meaning you'll need to return the car with a full tank of fuel.

Renting a car to explore the Highland routes and Isle of Skye gives you the ultimate freedom to enjoy the breathtaking beauty of Scotland at your own pace. With convenient pick-up locations, a range of car options, and access to scenic routes and remote destinations, a self-drive journey is an unforgettable way to experience the country's rugged charm. Whether you're heading to the Highlands, navigating the Isle of Skye, or simply enjoying a leisurely drive, having your own car opens up a world of adventure in Scotland.

Cycling and Walking Paths for Exploration in Scotland

Scotland offers an extensive network of cycling and walking paths, making it an ideal destination for outdoor enthusiasts. Whether you're looking to explore the country's stunning landscapes by bike or on foot, there's a trail for every level of fitness and interest. From scenic coastal routes to challenging mountain trails, Scotland's natural beauty can be experienced in an intimate way by following its diverse cycling and walking paths.

Cycling Paths for Exploration

Cycling is one of the best ways to explore Scotland's majestic scenery, offering routes that take you through everything from bustling cities to remote Highlands and serene coastal areas. Here are some of the top cycling paths:

- The North Coast 500 (NC500): A famous route that winds through the Scottish Highlands, the NC500 offers over 500 miles of roads with spectacular coastal views, remote villages, and dramatic landscapes. While it's typically done by car, it's also popular with cyclists looking for a more challenging adventure. The route includes quiet roads, hill climbs, and beautiful stretches by the sea.

- The Great Glen Way: This route stretches from Fort William to Inverness, following the Great Glen through stunning landscapes and picturesque lochs, including Loch Ness. While popular for walking, it's also a fantastic cycling route for those who want to explore Scotland's natural beauty at a leisurely pace.

- The Hebridean Way (Hebrides): For cyclists looking to explore the stunning Outer Hebrides, this 185-mile route covers the archipelago from Vatersay to Lewis, offering beautiful views of the Atlantic Ocean, sandy beaches, and historical sites. It's ideal for those who want to experience island life, with options for ferry crossings to access various islands.

- The Caledonia Way: Running from Campbeltown on the Kintyre Peninsula to Inverness, the Caledonia Way offers cyclists a journey through some of the most beautiful and rugged areas of Scotland. You'll pass through remote villages, wild landscapes, and coastal areas with panoramic views.

- The Clyde Coastal Path: This route follows the Clyde estuary along the west coast of Scotland, from the River Clyde to the Firth of Clyde. It's an ideal path for cycling, offering views of the river, the surrounding hills, and the opportunity to explore towns like Helensburgh and Gourock.

Walking Paths for Exploration

For those who prefer exploring on foot, Scotland offers a range of walking trails that take you through its most breathtaking scenery. Here are some popular walking routes:

- The West Highland Way: One of Scotland's most famous long-distance walks, the West Highland Way stretches 96 miles from Milngavie (near Glasgow) to Fort William. The trail takes walkers through rolling hills, tranquil lochs, and the rugged beauty of the Scottish Highlands. It's perfect for those seeking a multi-day adventure that offers a combination of natural beauty and physical challenge.

- The Fife Coastal Path: Running for over 80 miles along the Fife coast, this path offers spectacular views of the North Sea, charming seaside villages, and historic sites. The trail is relatively flat, making it suitable for both beginner and experienced walkers.

- The Southern Upland Way: This 212-mile trail runs from Portpatrick on the west coast to Cockburnspath on the east, crossing some of Scotland's most remote and dramatic landscapes. Walkers will experience coastal cliffs, deep valleys, and rolling hills while traversing through southern Scotland's rugged beauty.

- Ben Nevis and the Mountain Routes: For avid walkers and climbers, Scotland's mountains offer some of the best hiking opportunities. The most famous of these is Ben Nevis, the UK's highest peak. The Ben Nevis Path takes you to the summit for panoramic views of the surrounding areas, while other mountain routes like Schiehallion and The Cairngorms provide equally stunning challenges.

- The Cairngorms National Park: The Cairngorms is a prime location for both walking and cycling. The park offers a network of trails for all levels, from gentle walks around lochs to more challenging mountain treks. Whether you're looking for a short stroll or a long hike through the rugged landscapes of Scotland's largest national park, you'll find it here.

- The John Muir Way: Running from Helensburgh on the west coast to Dunbar on the east, this 134-mile route takes walkers through diverse landscapes, from forests and fields to coastlines and small towns. It's a great way to explore the country's natural beauty while learning about John Muir's legacy as a naturalist and conservationist.

- Loch Lomond and The Trossachs National Park: This national park offers a wide variety of walking paths, from peaceful lochside strolls to challenging mountain hikes. The West Highland Way passes through the park, but there are also shorter, easy-access walks, including those around Loch Katrine and Loch Lomond itself.

What to Expect

- Varied Terrain: Expect a diverse range of terrains, from coastal paths and forest walks to mountain trails and flat river routes. Many paths are well-maintained, but more rugged hikes may require sturdy boots, a good map, and preparation for changing weather.

- Stunning Views: The best part of cycling or walking in Scotland is the chance to take in some of the most dramatic landscapes in the world. Whether you're cycling by the sea, walking through ancient forests, or hiking in the mountains, the views will leave you in awe.

- Weather Variability: Be prepared for the weather to change quickly, especially in the Highlands. It's not uncommon for walkers and cyclists to experience rain, wind, and sunshine all in one day, so layering and waterproof clothing are essential.

- Wildlife Encounters: Depending on the area, you may encounter a variety of wildlife, including red deer, golden eagles, and otters. Many of the trails also pass through nature reserves, making them ideal for wildlife enthusiasts.

How to Get There

- Public Transport Access: Many of the walking and cycling routes are easily accessible by train, bus, or ferry. For example, the West Highland Way is easily accessible from Glasgow, while the Fife Coastal Path can be reached via public transport from Edinburgh.

- Car Access: Some of the more remote trails, especially in the Highlands or on the Isle of Skye, may require a car to reach the trailhead. Car rentals are available in major cities and transport hubs, and there are numerous parking facilities at popular starting points for cycling and walking routes.

Cost

- Walking Paths: Most walking paths in Scotland are free to access, although some specific routes, such as Ben Nevis, may require a small parking fee or donation. There may also be costs for guided walks or multi-day treks with accommodation.

- Cycling Paths: Similarly, many cycling routes are free to use, but renting a bike will incur costs. Prices for bike hire generally range from £20 to £40 per day, depending on the type of bike (standard, mountain, or electric). For guided cycling tours, prices can range from £50 to £100 per day.

- Additional Costs: For multi-day hikes or cycling trips, you'll need to factor in accommodation, food, and transport costs. Some trails, like the West Highland Way, offer a range of accommodation options along the route, from campsites to luxury hotels.

Scotland's cycling and walking paths offer a perfect way to explore its stunning landscapes, whether you're an avid cyclist or a leisurely walker. From the dramatic highlands to the peaceful coastline, there's a trail for everyone, providing opportunities for adventure, relaxation, and wildlife encounters. Whether you're traversing the rugged terrain of the Cairngorms or cycling along the serene shores of the Hebrides, Scotland's paths will lead you to unforgettable experiences in nature.

Tips for Driving in Rural and Remote Areas of Scotland

Driving through Scotland's rural and remote areas is an incredible way to experience the country's wild beauty, but it can present unique challenges due to the terrain, weather, and limited infrastructure. To ensure a safe and enjoyable journey, here are some essential tips for driving in Scotland's more remote locations, particularly in the Highlands and on the Isle of Skye.

1. Plan Your Route and Be Prepared

- Research Ahead: Many rural roads in Scotland can be narrow, winding, and less clearly marked than in urban areas. Make sure to plan your route ahead of time and have an up-to-date map or GPS system. Be aware of any road closures or delays due to weather or seasonal conditions.

- Check for Fuel Stations: Gas stations can be few and far between in remote regions. Plan your stops for fuel, especially in the Highlands or on smaller islands, where you might not find a station for miles. Always top up when you get the chance.

2. Be Ready for Narrow, Single-Track Roads

- Understand Single-Track Roads: Many rural roads, especially in the Highlands, are single-track, meaning only one vehicle can pass at a time. These roads are often lined with high stone walls, hedges, or rugged terrain, leaving little room to maneuver.

- Passing Places: Single-track roads have designated "passing places"—small pull-off areas where vehicles can stop and let others pass. If you see another car coming, slow down, and pull into a passing place to allow them to go by. It's courteous to wave when you're giving way.

- Speed: Keep your speed low on narrow roads to ensure you can stop in time for oncoming traffic. Be particularly cautious on bends or blind corners.

3. Be Aware of the Weather

- Unpredictable Conditions: Weather in Scotland can change rapidly, especially in the more remote regions. Heavy rain, fog, and snow are common, particularly in the winter months. Always check the forecast before setting out and keep an eye on conditions throughout the day.

- Prepare for Slippery Roads: In wet conditions, be mindful of slippery surfaces. Puddles can hide potholes, and icy patches can appear unexpectedly, especially in rural areas that may not be as frequently gritted as city roads.

- Visibility: Fog is common in certain areas, such as along lochs or in the Highlands. Ensure your headlights are on, reduce your speed, and keep a safe distance from other vehicles if visibility is poor.

4. Be Mindful of Wildlife and Livestock

- Wildlife Crossings: In rural areas, you may encounter wildlife, such as deer, red squirrels, or birds. Always remain alert, especially in twilight or nighttime hours when animals are most active. If you see wildlife near the road, slow down and be prepared to stop.

- Livestock on Roads: It's common to see cattle, sheep, or even horses grazing on or near the road, especially on rural farmland. Be cautious when driving through farming areas and keep an eye out for animals that might stray onto the road.

5. Check Your Car's Condition

- Tyre Pressure and Tread: Before heading to rural and remote areas, check the condition of your car, especially the tyres. The roads can be bumpy or uneven, and having good tyres with the right pressure will prevent accidents.

- Spare Tyre: Carry a spare tyre and the tools needed to change it in case of an emergency. In some remote locations, roadside assistance may take longer to arrive.

6. Keep Emergency Supplies

- First Aid Kit: Always carry a basic first aid kit, just in case of minor injuries or emergencies.

- Water and Snacks: It's a good idea to have a bottle of water and some snacks with you, especially if you're venturing into areas with little to no services. You may be driving for long stretches without access to food or drink.

- Charged Phone: Ensure your phone is fully charged and have a portable charger handy. In more remote areas, mobile phone signals can be weak or nonexistent, so consider informing someone of your travel plans in case you lose contact.

7. Take Extra Care in Highland and Coastal Areas

- Highland Terrain: When driving in the Highlands, expect lots of hills, bends, and highland moorlands. Be prepared for frequent ascents and descents, and always use your brakes wisely on downhill stretches.

- Coastal Roads: Coastal routes, such as the North Coast 500, can offer breathtaking views, but they can also be treacherous. Watch out for cliffs, sudden drops, and coastal winds. Some roads may be narrow, winding, and exposed, with little barrier protection.

8. Stay Alert for Construction and Roadworks

- Seasonal Roadworks: Roadworks can occur on rural roads, especially in the summer months when tourism is at its peak. Look out for signs indicating slow-moving traffic or construction zones. Be patient, as you may have to wait for other vehicles to pass.

- Diversions: If you're following a GPS or sat-nav, be mindful of road diversions due to construction. Some rural roads are less frequently updated, so double-check on local traffic apps or news for the latest detours.

9. Drive on the Left

- Left-Hand Driving: In Scotland, as with the rest of the UK, vehicles drive on the left side of the road. This can be a bit of a challenge for those accustomed to driving on the right. When in doubt, pay extra attention to road signs and traffic markings, and practice on quieter roads before tackling busier routes.

10. Driving at Night

- Night Driving: Driving in rural areas at night can be daunting, especially due to the absence of streetlights and possible wildlife crossing the road. If you're not comfortable driving in the dark, try to plan your routes during daylight hours.

- Headlights: Always use your headlights in low visibility or dark conditions. In rural areas, other vehicles may not have their lights on, so stay extra vigilant.

11. Be Courteous to Locals

- Respect Local Driving Habits: Scots are generally patient drivers, and many are used to navigating remote roads. If you need to pull over to let someone pass, always do so in a safe and considerate manner.

- Road Etiquette: On single-track roads, give way to vehicles coming from the opposite direction. It's customary to wave a friendly acknowledgment when passing others on the road.

Driving in Scotland's rural and remote areas can be an unforgettable experience, offering some of the most scenic and peaceful routes in the world. However, it does come with its own set of challenges, from narrow roads and unpredictable weather to wildlife encounters and limited services. By staying prepared, driving cautiously, and respecting the environment, you can make the most of your journey through this breathtaking landscape.

Chapter 10: Sample Itinerary and Travel Tips

7-Day Itinerary: Edinburgh, Stirling, Glasgow, The Highlands, Isle of Skye, and St. Andrews

7-Day Itinerary: Edinburgh, Stirling, Glasgow, The Highlands, Isle of Skye, and St. Andrews

Scotland offers a wealth of history, stunning landscapes, and vibrant culture, and a 7-day itinerary allows you to explore some of the country's most iconic cities and natural wonders. From the grandeur of Edinburgh Castle to the rugged beauty of the Isle of Skye, this itinerary ensures you experience the best of Scotland's history, cities, and landscapes. Below is a recommended 7-day itinerary that will take you through Edinburgh, Stirling, Glasgow, the Highlands, the Isle of Skye, and St. Andrews.

Day 1: Arrival in Edinburgh

What to Expect: Arrive in Edinburgh and dive into Scotland's capital, a city rich in history, culture, and stunning architecture. Edinburgh is famed for its medieval Old Town, beautiful parks, and lively festivals.

Highlights:

- Edinburgh Castle: Begin your adventure with a visit to this historic fortress. Explore the Crown Jewels, St. Margaret's Chapel, and the Stone of Destiny.

- Royal Mile: Walk along this iconic street from the Castle to the Palace of Holyroodhouse, passing historic sites, shops, and restaurants.

- Arthur's Seat: End the day with a hike up this dormant volcano for stunning views over the city.

What to Explore:

- National Museum of Scotland

- Greyfriars Kirk and the famous Greyfriars Bobby statue

- The Scotch Whisky Experience

Cost: Entrance to Edinburgh Castle is around £19, Arthur's Seat is free to climb, and most museums are free or have a nominal entry fee.

Day 2: Stirling - History and Heritage

What to Expect: Drive to Stirling, a small city packed with history. Stirling Castle, a pivotal site in Scottish history, is a must-see, along with the surrounding medieval streets.

Highlights:

- Stirling Castle: Explore one of Scotland's most important castles, which was home to many Scottish kings and queens, including Mary, Queen of Scots.

- Wallace Monument: Pay tribute to William Wallace at this iconic tower offering panoramic views of the surrounding countryside.

- Battle of Stirling Bridge Site: Learn about the famous battle of 1297 where Wallace led his troops to victory.

What to Explore:

- The Old Town and its medieval architecture

- Stirling's beautiful parks and the River Forth

How to Get There:

- A 1-hour drive from Edinburgh.

Cost: Stirling Castle entry is around £16, Wallace Monument is approximately £7.

Day 3: Glasgow – Scotland's Cultural Hub

What to Expect: Head to Glasgow, Scotland's largest city known for its art, music, and vibrant nightlife. The city boasts impressive museums, architecture, and green spaces.

Highlights:

- Kelvingrove Art Gallery and Museum: Explore Glasgow's most popular museum, housing everything from fine art to natural history.

- Glasgow Cathedral: Visit this stunning medieval cathedral and nearby Necropolis for views over the city.

- Buchanan Street: Enjoy shopping and stroll through this pedestrianized street lined with shops, cafes, and restaurants.

What to Explore:

- The Glasgow School of Art (designed by Charles Rennie Mackintosh)

- Glasgow Botanic Gardens

How to Get There:

- 1-hour drive from Stirling.

Cost: Kelvingrove Art Gallery is free, Glasgow Cathedral entry is free with a suggested donation.

Day 4: The Highlands – Nature's Beauty

What to Expect: Embark on your journey through the Scottish Highlands, home to breathtaking landscapes, towering mountains, and serene lochs. A drive through the Highlands offers some of Scotland's most scenic views.

Highlights:

•	Loch Lomond: Stop for a stroll or boat ride around Scotland's largest loch, surrounded by the towering peaks of the Trossachs.

•	Ben Nevis: Hike or admire the tallest mountain in the UK.

•	Glen Coe: This dramatic valley is a must-see, known for its eerie beauty and historical significance.

What to Explore:

•	Highland villages such as Fort William and Glencoe

•	The Caledonian Canal

How to Get There:

•	2.5-hour drive from Glasgow.

Cost: Loch Lomond boat tours cost around £15, hiking in Glen Coe is free.

Day 5: Isle of Skye – Majestic Landscapes

What to Expect: Drive to the Isle of Skye, one of Scotland's most iconic islands, known for its dramatic landscapes, cliffs, and fairy-tale-like scenery. The Isle of Skye is a paradise for nature lovers and adventure seekers.

Highlights:

•	Fairy Pools: Hike to these famous pools near Glen Brittle, renowned for their crystal-clear waters.

•	Old Man of Storr: Hike to this famous rocky pinnacle for panoramic views.

•	Dunvegan Castle: Explore this historic castle and its beautiful gardens, the ancestral home of the MacLeod clan.

What to Explore:

•	The Quiraing, a stunning area for hiking and photography

- Neist Point Lighthouse for spectacular coastal views

How to Get There:

- 4-hour drive from the Highlands.

Cost: Entry to Dunvegan Castle is around £13, most hikes are free.

Day 6: St. Andrews – Golf, History, and Coastal Beauty

What to Expect: Drive east to St. Andrews, a town known for its ancient university, golf course, and coastal beauty. It's also one of the most picturesque towns in Scotland.

Highlights:

- St. Andrews Castle: Explore the ruins of this historic castle perched on the cliffs.

- St. Andrews Cathedral: Walk around the remains of Scotland's largest cathedral and enjoy the views over the North Sea.

- The Old Course: If you're a golfer, you can visit the world-famous Old Course, or simply enjoy the surrounding area.

What to Explore:

- The town's charming streets lined with cafes and boutiques

- West Sands Beach, famous for its role in the film Chariots of Fire

How to Get There:

- 1.5-hour drive from the Isle of Skye.

Cost: Entry to St. Andrews Castle is around £6, the Old Course is free to walk around, but green fees for golf can be expensive.

Day 7: Return to Edinburgh

What to Expect: On your final day, drive back to Edinburgh for a relaxed exploration of any sites you missed on Day 1. Depending on your time, you may also want to explore some additional spots or relax before your departure.

Highlights:

- The Royal Yacht Britannia: Visit this former royal yacht now moored in Leith, showcasing life aboard the royal family's floating residence.

- Calton Hill: For stunning panoramic views of Edinburgh, climb Calton Hill and admire the neoclassical monuments.

What to Explore:

- Princes Street Gardens and shopping districts
- Local markets, cafes, and the vibrant nightlife

How to Get There:

- 1-hour drive from St. Andrews to Edinburgh.

Cost: The Royal Yacht Britannia entry is around £14.

This 7-day itinerary takes you on a whirlwind tour of Scotland's most iconic cities and stunning landscapes. From the vibrant culture of Edinburgh and Glasgow to the serene beauty of the Highlands and Isle of Skye, you'll experience the diverse charm that makes Scotland a truly special destination.

How to Plan Your Trip to Scotland for Different Seasons

Scotland is a beautiful destination year-round, but the experience can vary dramatically depending on when you visit. Each season brings unique weather patterns, activities, and events, making it essential to plan accordingly. Below is a guide to help you make the most of your trip, no matter the season.

Spring (March to May)

What to Expect:

- Weather: Spring in Scotland can be quite unpredictable, with cool temperatures and occasional rainfall. Expect average temperatures between 5°C (41°F) and 15°C (59°F). However, the days begin to lengthen, and the countryside starts to bloom, providing a vibrant backdrop.

- What to Explore: Spring is the best time to enjoy the blooming of Scotland's wildflowers, gardens, and forests. The Isle of Skye and the Highlands are particularly picturesque during this time. Visit the famous Royal Botanic Garden in Edinburgh, or go hiking in Cairngorms National Park where the snow starts to melt, revealing spectacular views.

- Festivals and Events: Look out for Edinburgh's International Science Festival and The Scottish Snowdrop Festival in early spring, both of which are ideal for those interested in culture and nature.

- What to Pack: Pack for varying weather. Light layers, waterproof jackets, warm clothes, and sturdy boots are recommended. Don't forget an umbrella or rain gear.

Activities to Consider:

- Outdoor hikes in the Highlands and Cairngorms
- Exploring gardens and nature trails
- Whale-watching tours along the coast

Summer (June to August)

What to Expect:

•   Weather: Summer in Scotland is typically mild and much warmer than other seasons, with temperatures ranging from 13°C (55°F) to 20°C (68°F). It's the driest time of year, although rainfall can still occur, particularly in the west and Highlands.

•   What to Explore: Summer is the best time to explore Scotland's rugged landscapes, including the Isle of Skye, Loch Ness, and the Outer Hebrides. Longer daylight hours (up to 16 hours a day) mean more time to explore. Hiking trails and coastal paths are ideal for walking, cycling, and exploring Scotland's historic castles, such as Edinburgh Castle and Urquhart Castle.

•   Festivals and Events: This is the season for festivals, with the Edinburgh Festival Fringe, The Royal Edinburgh Military Tattoo, and The Highland Games taking place across the country. These events bring Scotland's culture, arts, and traditions to life.

•   What to Pack: Light layers, comfortable walking shoes, sunscreen, sunglasses, and a rain jacket are a must.

Activities to Consider:

•   Attend the Edinburgh Festival Fringe for an arts experience

•   Go on a scenic road trip through the Scottish Highlands

•   Take part in the Highland Games in various regions

Autumn (September to November)

What to Expect:

•   Weather: Autumn in Scotland brings cooler temperatures (averaging 9°C/48°F to 15°C/59°F) and a chance of rainfall. The weather can be windy and crisp, but the fall foliage makes it a visually stunning time to visit.

•   What to Explore: Autumn is the best time for scenic drives, particularly through the Highlands, where the vibrant autumn colors are in full display. Popular spots like Cairngorms National Park and Glencoe are breathtaking with their red, orange, and golden hues. It's also the perfect time to enjoy quiet walks in the countryside or visit historic sites like Stirling Castle.

•   Festivals and Events: The Edinburgh International Festival of Literature and The Scottish International Storytelling Festival are great for those interested in literature and culture. Autumn also brings harvest festivals and food events, perfect for foodies.

•   What to Pack: Bring warm layers, a waterproof jacket, and sturdy shoes for walking or hiking. It's also good to pack an umbrella for rain showers.

Activities to Consider:

- Explore Loch Lomond & The Trossachs National Park for the fall colors
- Visit Edinburgh's Royal Botanic Garden for autumn displays
- Take a whisky tour to celebrate the harvest season

Winter (December to February)

What to Expect:

- Weather: Winter in Scotland is cold, with temperatures typically ranging from 0°C (32°F) to 5°C (41°F), although it can dip below freezing in the north and in the Highlands. Snow is common in the mountains and more remote areas.

- What to Explore: Winter is the season for cozying up in pubs, enjoying whisky tastings, and experiencing Scotland's festive atmosphere. You can also enjoy outdoor activities like skiing or snowboarding in Cairngorms National Park or Glencoe. Major cities like Edinburgh and Glasgow are festive during the holiday season, with Christmas markets, light displays, and winter festivals.

- Festivals and Events: Hogmanay (New Year's Eve) in Edinburgh is world-famous for its incredible street parties, fireworks, and celebrations. Burns Night in January also brings traditional Scottish food, music, and poetry.

- What to Pack: Pack warm clothes, including thermals, a heavy coat, scarves, gloves, and waterproof footwear for snow or rain.

Activities to Consider:

- Celebrate Hogmanay in Edinburgh
- Skiing or snowboarding in the Scottish Highlands
- Enjoy a whisky distillery tour during the colder months

General Tips for Every Season

- Book in Advance: Some of Scotland's most popular destinations, like Edinburgh and the Isle of Skye, can get crowded, especially during summer. It's wise to book your accommodations and some tours in advance, particularly if you're visiting during the festival season.

- Pack for Changing Weather: Scotland's weather is famously unpredictable. Regardless of the season, bring layers and be prepared for occasional rain. Always pack a waterproof jacket and sturdy shoes, especially if you plan on hiking.

- Accommodation Choices: In spring and autumn, you may find more affordable options for accommodation compared to peak summer months. Winter offers plenty of cozy, warm places to stay with fewer crowds.

- Local Events: Many local festivals and events are based around the seasons, like the Whisky Festivals in autumn or the Scotch Whisky Experience year-round. Check event calendars ahead of your trip to see what special events might be happening during your visit.

Scotland offers something special in every season. Whether you're hiking the rugged Highlands in summer, enjoying the colorful landscapes of autumn, or attending a festive Hogmanay celebration in Edinburgh, each season brings a unique experience. By planning your trip according to the weather and events, you can ensure a memorable and rewarding visit to Scotland.

Packing Tips and Essential Items to Bring for Your Trip to Scotland

Scotland's diverse landscapes, unpredictable weather, and rich cultural experiences make it essential to pack wisely for your trip. Whether you're exploring the cities, hiking in the Highlands, or touring castles and distilleries, here's a comprehensive guide to packing the essentials for your Scottish adventure.

Weather-Ready Clothing

Scotland's weather is notoriously changeable, so it's crucial to pack clothes that will keep you comfortable in any conditions. Here's what to bring:

- Layered Clothing: Scotland's weather can shift rapidly, so layering is key. Pack a mix of light, breathable layers for warmer days and thicker layers for colder weather.

- Waterproof Jacket: Rain is common year-round, especially in the west and the Highlands. A lightweight, breathable waterproof jacket will keep you dry without overheating.

- Warm Layers: Even in summer, temperatures can dip, particularly in the evenings or in the Highlands. A fleece or thermal layer is perfect for these conditions.

- Scarf, Hat, and Gloves: These accessories are essential, especially if you're visiting during the colder months. A warm hat and gloves will keep you cozy in chilly weather.

- Comfortable Walking Shoes: Whether you're exploring cities, hiking in the hills, or walking along coastal paths, comfortable waterproof walking shoes are a must. Choose shoes that can handle muddy terrain or cobbled streets.

- Sun Protection: Although Scotland can be rainy, you should still bring sunglasses, sunscreen, and a hat for protection on sunny days, particularly if you plan on spending time outdoors.

Hiking and Outdoor Gear

Scotland is a haven for outdoor enthusiasts, offering everything from gentle coastal walks to challenging mountain hikes. If you're planning to explore Scotland's wilderness, pack the following items:

- Hiking Boots: Waterproof, sturdy hiking boots are essential for trekking across the Highlands, walking along coastal paths, or navigating rocky terrains on the Isle of Skye.

- Backpack: A comfortable, lightweight daypack will help you carry water, snacks, and other essentials while hiking.

- Water Bottle: Scotland's landscapes are best enjoyed outdoors, so a reusable water bottle will help keep you hydrated during hikes.

- Trekking Poles: For those tackling more strenuous hikes, trekking poles can provide added stability and reduce the strain on your joints.

- Binoculars and Camera: Scotland's scenery is breathtaking, so a camera or smartphone with extra memory is essential to capture the stunning views. If you're into wildlife watching, binoculars are a great addition.

Travel Essentials

Be sure to pack the basics that will make your journey smooth and enjoyable:

- Passport/ID: You'll need a passport for international travel, and a driver's license if you plan to rent a car.

- Travel Insurance: Always bring a copy of your travel insurance, particularly if you're hiking or taking part in adventurous activities like skiing or watersports.

- Cash and Cards: While credit cards are widely accepted, it's a good idea to carry some local currency (British pounds) for smaller purchases, especially in rural areas or smaller shops.

- Guidebook/Maps: Although smartphones and GPS are handy, a physical guidebook or map is useful when exploring remote areas with limited service.

- Power Adapters/Chargers: The UK uses a specific type of plug (Type G) with three rectangular prongs, so pack a travel adapter if you're coming from outside the UK.

- Phone and SIM Card/International Roaming: To stay connected, consider purchasing a UK SIM card or activating an international plan for your phone.

Toiletries and Health Supplies

Scotland offers plenty of modern amenities, but some basic items are still important to pack:

- Travel Toiletries Kit: Many accommodations provide basic toiletries, but it's always a good idea to carry your own essentials (shampoo, conditioner, toothpaste, deodorant) in travel-sized containers.

- Sunscreen and Lip Balm: Even in winter, the sun's reflection off snow or the sea can cause sunburn. Protect your skin with a good sunscreen and lip balm with SPF.

- Medications/First Aid Kit: If you take prescription medications, make sure to bring enough for your entire trip. It's also a good idea to pack a basic first aid kit, including plasters, antiseptic, painkillers, and any other personal items.

- Insect Repellent: In summer months, midges (small biting insects) are common in the Highlands, especially in remote areas. A good insect repellent is essential to avoid bites.

Food and Snacks

Scotland is known for its delicious cuisine, but it's always handy to bring some of your own supplies, particularly for longer journeys:

- Snacks for Hiking: High-energy snacks like trail mix, granola bars, or dried fruit are ideal for hiking trips in remote areas where shops might be scarce.

- Reusable Food Containers: If you're planning on picnicking, a small set of reusable containers or a cooler bag for your lunch can come in handy.

- Tote Bag: Scotland is eco-friendly, and many shops charge for plastic bags. Pack a reusable tote bag for carrying groceries or items purchased during your travels.

Electronics and Entertainment

Scotland's long journeys and stunning landscapes mean you'll want to keep yourself entertained during travel and downtime:

- Camera/Smartphone: You'll want to capture every moment, so a camera with extra memory cards or a smartphone with ample storage is essential.

- Chargers and Power Bank: Long days of sightseeing and outdoor adventures will quickly drain your devices. Pack chargers for your devices, plus a portable power bank for recharging on the go.

- Books, E-Reader, or Journals: Scotland's natural beauty makes it a great place for reading or journaling. Whether it's a book, a Kindle, or a notebook, bring something to pass the time during quiet moments.

- Travel Pillow and Eye Mask: For long bus, train, or flight journeys, these can make travel more comfortable.

Travel Extras

Depending on your interests, you may want to bring:

- Whisky Tasting Guidebook: If you're keen on whisky, bring a guidebook or app to help you identify distilleries, or consider booking a whisky tour.

- Fishing Gear: Scotland is home to some of Europe's best fishing spots. If you're planning on fishing, be sure to bring your own gear or check if rentals are available.

- Golf Equipment: Scotland is the birthplace of golf, so if you plan to hit the greens, bring your golf clubs or check for rental options at world-famous courses like St Andrews.

Packing for Scotland requires a balance between preparing for its ever-changing weather and making sure you're ready to explore its rugged landscapes and bustling cities. By following these tips and packing the essentials, you'll be well-equipped to enjoy everything Scotland has to offer. Remember to leave some room for souvenirs, as Scotland is full of delightful treasures to bring home.

Navigating Scotland's Weather and Terrain

Scotland's weather and terrain are some of the most distinctive features of the country. With its varied landscapes, from rugged coastlines and rolling hills to towering mountains and vast forests, the weather can change dramatically within a single day. Understanding Scotland's weather patterns and terrain is key to making the most of your travels. Here's a detailed guide to navigating these elements so you can explore the country with confidence and comfort.

Understanding Scotland's Weather

Scotland's weather is famously unpredictable. The country is located at a high latitude, and its proximity to the Atlantic Ocean means it experiences frequent rainfall, particularly in the west and in mountainous regions. However, Scotland also has its fair share of sunshine and clear skies, especially during the summer months.

Weather Seasons

Winter (December to February):

- Temperature: Winter temperatures in Scotland can be cold, especially in the Highlands and the far north. On average, temperatures hover between 0°C and 5°C (32°F - 41°F), though they can drop lower in the mountains.

- What to Expect: Snowfall is common, particularly in higher altitudes. Coastal areas, however, are milder but can be quite wet and windy.

- What to Wear: Layering is key in winter. Bring thermal undergarments, insulated jackets, waterproof clothing, gloves, hats, and sturdy footwear to keep warm and dry.

Spring (March to May):

- Temperature: Temperatures begin to rise but can still be unpredictable, ranging from 5°C to 15°C (41°F - 59°F).

- What to Expect: Spring is a time of transition, with the possibility of rain showers and the occasional sunny day. It's also when the countryside begins to bloom, making it a great time to visit.

- What to Wear: A waterproof jacket is a must, along with layers to adjust to changing temperatures. Sturdy shoes are still important as the ground may be wet.

Summer (June to August):

- Temperature: Summer temperatures in Scotland are relatively mild, ranging from 10°C to 20°C (50°F - 68°F), although it can sometimes reach higher temperatures during heatwaves.

- What to Expect: While rain is still a possibility, summer offers the best weather for outdoor activities like hiking and sightseeing. The days are long, with daylight lasting until 10 p.m. in some parts of the country.

- What to Wear: Light layers, a waterproof jacket, and sunscreen are essential. Be prepared for occasional showers even in the summer.

Autumn (September to November):

- Temperature: Autumn sees a gradual decrease in temperatures, averaging between 5°C and 15°C (41°F - 59°F).

- What to Expect: Scotland's landscape takes on vibrant autumnal colors, with the leaves changing to shades of orange, red, and yellow. Rain and wind can pick up, particularly as the season progresses.

- What to Wear: Bring layers to adjust to the fluctuating temperatures. A good waterproof jacket and sturdy shoes will be necessary, especially if you plan to hike or explore rural areas.

Microclimates Across Scotland

Scotland's varied terrain creates microclimates, where the weather can vary considerably from one region to another. Some key regions to consider:

- The West Coast & Islands: The west coast and islands, such as the Isle of Skye, tend to be wetter due to the moist air from the Atlantic. The weather here is more unpredictable, with heavy rain and winds common throughout the year.

- The Highlands: The Highlands are more mountainous, so the weather can be more extreme. Expect colder temperatures, particularly at higher altitudes, and the potential for snow in winter.

- The Lowlands & Central Belt: The area around Glasgow, Stirling, and Edinburgh is relatively milder but still experiences frequent rain. This region is ideal for city sightseeing and urban exploration, especially during the summer.

- The North & Northeast: The weather in the far north can be harsher, with colder temperatures and stronger winds. This is the perfect place for those seeking more rugged and remote environments.

Navigating Scotland's Terrain

Scotland's terrain is as varied as its weather, offering everything from coastal cliffs and lochs to rolling hills and snow-capped mountains. Understanding the landscape is essential for any outdoor adventure.

The Highlands

The Scottish Highlands are one of the most iconic parts of the country. Known for their towering mountains, such as Ben Nevis (the UK's highest peak), vast glens, and pristine lochs, the Highlands offer some of the best hiking, mountain biking, and scenic drives in Scotland.

- Terrain: The Highlands are rugged and remote, with plenty of challenges for experienced hikers and adventurers. There are also more accessible routes for those new to outdoor exploration.

- What to Expect: Hikers will face steep inclines, rocky paths, and sometimes even boggy ground. The weather can change quickly in the Highlands, so be prepared for rain, wind, and sudden temperature drops.

- Getting Around: The terrain is best explored by foot or by car. If you're hiking, make sure you have proper footwear and a map, as some paths are not clearly marked.

The Islands

Scotland's islands offer a mix of dramatic coastlines and tranquil seascapes. Popular islands like the Isle of Skye, the Orkney Islands, and the Outer Hebrides are all accessible by ferry.

- Terrain: Island terrain can vary from sandy beaches to rugged cliffs, with rocky hills and ancient ruins to explore. The weather on the islands can be unpredictable, especially in winter, with strong winds and rain.

- What to Expect: On islands like Skye, you'll find dramatic vistas, hidden coves, and historical sites, as well as a variety of wildlife. The terrain can be challenging, so it's advisable to check the weather before heading out for a hike.

- Getting Around: Ferries are the primary mode of transport to the islands. Once on the island, many areas are accessible by car, bike, or on foot.

The Lowlands

The Lowlands are a flatter, more fertile region in central Scotland, perfect for cycling and hiking.

- Terrain: The terrain here is more gentle, with rolling hills and rivers ideal for kayaking or canoeing. The Lowlands are also home to some of Scotland's most historic cities, such as Edinburgh and Glasgow.

- What to Expect: Expect to encounter well-maintained paths and scenic routes, especially along the River Clyde or through areas like the Trossachs National Park.

- Getting Around: The Lowlands are well connected by roads and public transport, making it easy to travel between cities and rural areas.

Tips for Navigating Scotland's Weather and Terrain

- Be Prepared for Sudden Changes: Always check the weather forecast before heading out for the day, especially in the Highlands or remote areas, where conditions can change rapidly.

- Wear the Right Gear: Layering is key in Scotland. Make sure you have waterproof and windproof clothing, sturdy footwear, and outdoor gear if you plan to hike or explore rural areas.

- Know Your Limits: Scotland's terrain can be challenging. If you're planning a hike or outdoor activity, choose routes that match your fitness level, and don't forget to take plenty of water and snacks.

- Respect the Environment: Scotland's natural beauty is one of its biggest draws. Make sure to follow the Scottish Outdoor Access Code to preserve the environment for future generations.

Scotland's weather and terrain are as diverse as its culture and history. Whether you're exploring the urban streets of Edinburgh or hiking through the remote Highlands, understanding what to expect in terms of weather and landscape will help you enjoy your trip to the fullest. Be sure to pack accordingly, and always be prepared for the unexpected!

Chapter 11. Conclusion

Reflecting on Scotland's Unforgettable Experience: A Journey Through Time, Nature, and Culture

Scotland is more than just a place; it's an experience—a blend of breathtaking landscapes, a rich tapestry of history, and a vibrant culture that touches every corner of the nation. Reflecting on a journey through Scotland, one can't help but be struck by the deep connection between past and present, nature and culture, and the legacy that continues to shape the country.

From the bustling streets of Edinburgh and Glasgow to the tranquility of the Highlands and Isle of Skye, Scotland offers a unique mix of urban sophistication and rural beauty. Edinburgh's cobbled streets tell stories of centuries past, where the grandeur of Edinburgh Castle stands tall, guarding the city's history. The Royal Mile offers glimpses into Scotland's storied past, while modern-day festivals and a thriving arts scene blend seamlessly with its ancient heritage. Each step through the city brings a deeper understanding of Scotland's long and illustrious history.

The landscapes of Scotland are equally unforgettable. The towering peaks of the Highlands, the serene waters of Loch Ness, and the coastal beauty of the Isle of Skye provide a rich natural environment perfect for adventure and quiet reflection. Whether hiking through Cairngorms National Park or taking a boat ride on Loch Lomond, the awe-inspiring views seem to stretch forever, offering the opportunity to connect with nature in its purest form. These landscapes, timeless and ever-changing, reflect the heart and soul of the Scottish people—resilient, proud, and deeply tied to the land.

Culturally, Scotland is a nation steeped in tradition, yet full of modern creativity. Its rich folklore, from the legend of the Loch Ness Monster to the tales of Scottish kings and warriors, is woven into the daily lives of its people. Scottish cuisine, too, reflects this blending of old and new, with classic dishes like haggis and Cullen Skink being enjoyed alongside modern food innovations. The warmth and hospitality of the Scottish people add an extra layer to the journey, inviting travelers to experience not just a country but a way of life.

Throughout your trip, you'll also encounter festivals and events that celebrate Scotland's culture in all its forms, from the world-renowned Edinburgh Festival Fringe to the lively Hogmanay celebrations on New Year's Eve. These events offer a glimpse into the joy, passion, and exuberance that define the Scottish spirit. It's in these moments of celebration that Scotland's vibrancy truly comes to life, making it clear why this is a country that people return to time and time again.

Scotland's unforgettable charm is also found in the smaller moments—the quiet stroll through the glens of the Highlands, the taste of a single malt whisky from a local distillery, or the magic of watching the sun set behind the hills of the Isle of Skye. It's a place where every corner holds a story, every landscape has its own beauty, and every moment feels like an adventure waiting to unfold.

As you reflect on your journey through Scotland, it becomes clear that this is a place that leaves an indelible mark on the heart. Scotland's ability to blend its rich history with its stunning natural beauty and vibrant culture creates an experience that is truly unique. Whether you've come for the history, the landscapes, or the warm hospitality, Scotland offers a journey that will stay with you long after you leave.

It's a country that invites exploration, sparks curiosity, and leaves you with memories that will last a lifetime.

Bonus

Travel Journal

Date	Destination /Stop	Key Activities/Excursions	Memorable Moments	Food Tried/Restaurants	Thoughts & Reflections	Photos Taken (Yes/No)
Day 1						
Day 2						
Day 3						
Day 4						
Day 5						
Day 6						
Day 7						
Packing List:		Special Memories to Remember:			Important Contacts/Information	

Dear Reader,

If you've enjoyed this travel guide and found the information useful in planning your trip to Scotland, I would deeply appreciate your positive feedback and review. As a travel guide writer, your review means more than just words to me—it's a testament to the effort and passion I've put into crafting this book, and it plays a significant role in my continued growth and development in this field.

Writing this guide has been a labor of love, involving not only countless hours of research but also personal visits to the places I've written about. I've invested my own time, energy, and resources to explore Scotland's stunning landscapes, rich history, and vibrant culture. Every piece of advice, every suggestion, and every recommendation has been carefully gathered to ensure you get the most out of your trip. Your positive review will not only help me to continue writing guides that are meaningful and helpful but also inspire others to explore the beauty that Scotland has to offer.

I truly hope this guide has enhanced your journey and provided the insight you need to experience Scotland in a way that is unforgettable. Your feedback not only motivates me but also helps others who are planning their own adventures to find the resources they need to make their travels truly remarkable.

Thank you for being a part of this journey with me. Your review is not just a kind gesture; it's an essential step in my progress as a travel writer, and it ensures that I can continue to share valuable content for fellow travelers.

Warm regards,

Darrin C. Ervin

Made in United States
Cleveland, OH
19 February 2025